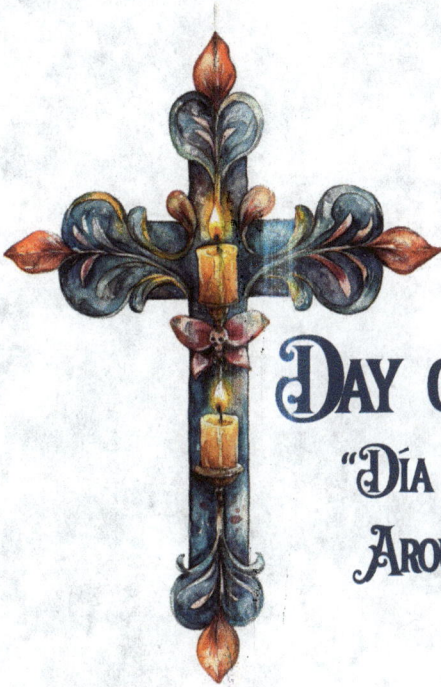

Honoring
Day of the Dead
"Día de los Muertos"
Around the World

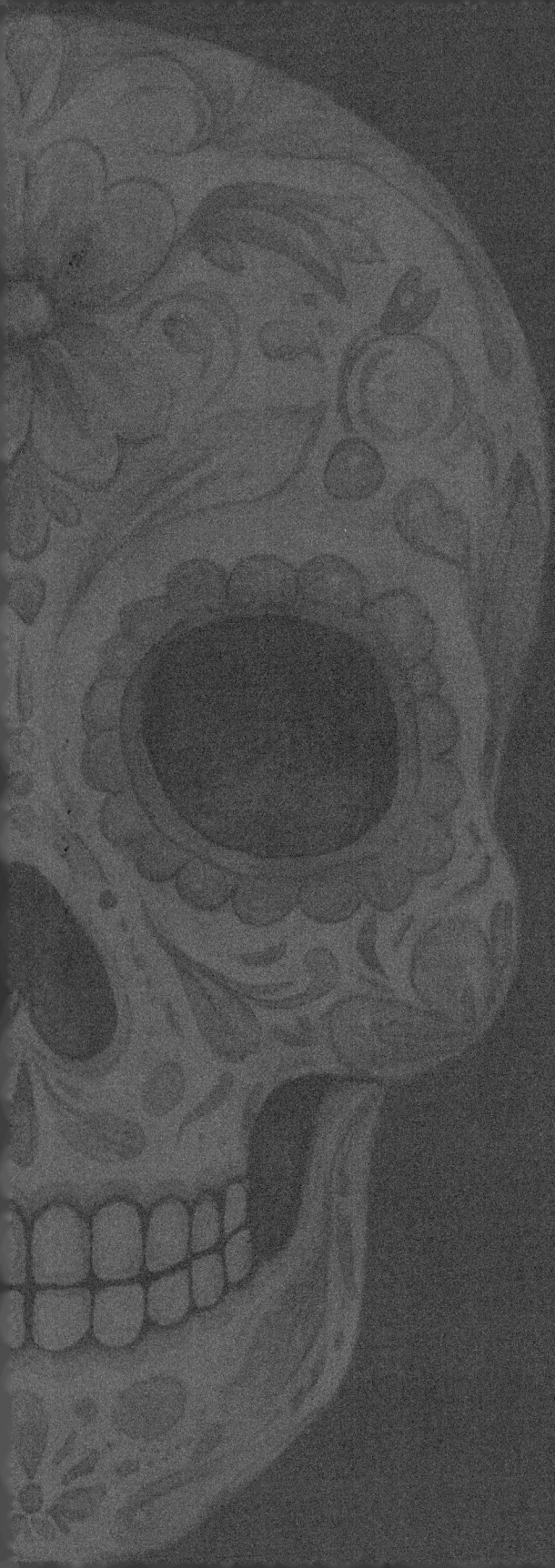

HONORING

DAY OF THE DEAD

"DÍA DE LOS MUERTOS" AROUND THE WORLD

DANIEL T. SANCHEZ

MANY**SEASONS**PRESS

Mesa, Arizona • 2025

FIRST EDITION

Honoring Day of the Dead "Día de los Muertos" Around the World

Copyright © 2025 Daniel T. Sanchez

✦

MANY**SEASONS**PRESS

Published by Many Seasons Press
an Imprint of Multimedia Publishing Project
123 N. Centennial Way, Suite 105
Mesa, Arizona 85201
480-939-9689 | MultimediaPublishingProject.com

Book designed by Yolie Hernandez
(AZBookDesigner@icloud.com)

Paperback ISBN: 978-1-956203-75-2

Library of Congress Control Number: 2025947923

Printed in the United States of America.

CONTENTS

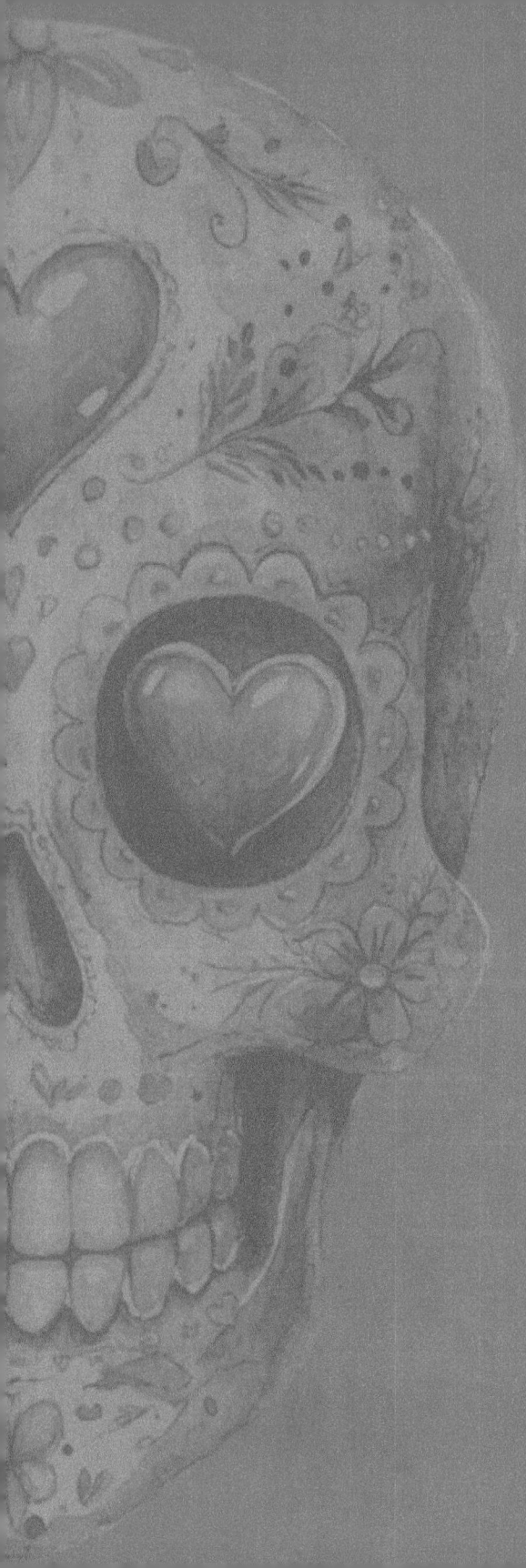

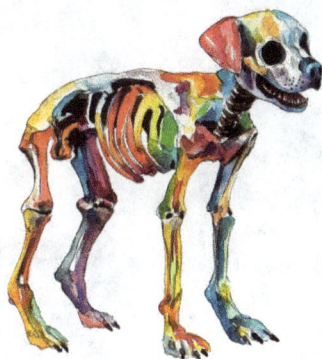

Acknowledgments

I WOULD LIKE TO EXPRESS MY GRATITUDE TO MY FAMILY AND FRIENDS FOR their guidance and support throughout the completion of this book

To my wife Mona and our family, who have always supported me.

Special thanks to Dr. Loui Olivas for his invaluable assistance in helping me write this book. He retired as a Colonel from the Arizona Air National Guard after 29 years of service and currently serves as the Commander of the American Legion Tony F. Soza-Ray Martinez Thunderbird Post 41 in Phoenix, Arizona.

To my publishers, Yolie Hernandez and Eduardo Barraza, of Many Seasons Press. who have also published my three previous books: *39 Years of Blue, A Collection of Life Stories, Hispanic Heritage and Participation on United States Stamps*, (acquired by the Smithsonian Institution Library and Archives in Washington, D.C.), and *Latino Medal of Honor from 1864-2011.*

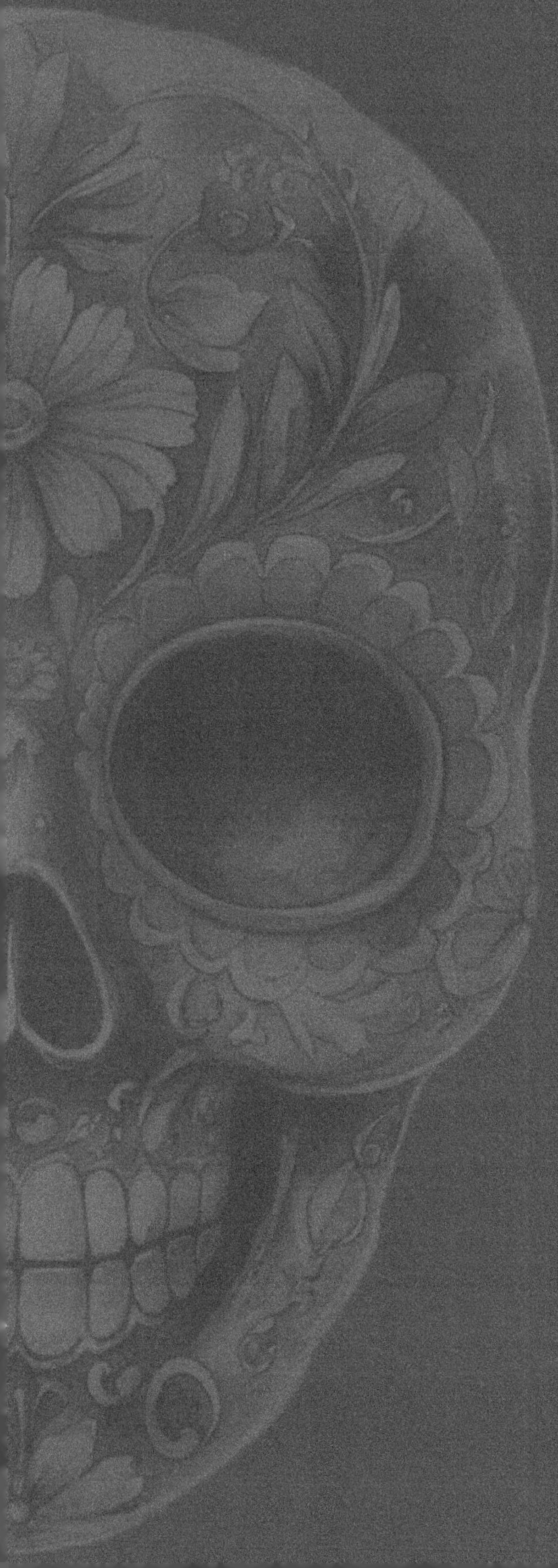

Day of the Dead
"Día de los Muertos"

Honoring the Lives of the Departed Across Cultures

OBSERVED IN MANY PARTS OF THE WORLD OVER SEVEN SPECIAL DAYS, Day of the Dead or *Día de los Muertos* begins on October 28 and ends on November 3. During this time, families visit cemeteries to remember, celebrate, and honor their departed loved ones.

Each of the seven days carries a specific meaning, though many people are only familiar with the celebrations on November 1 and 2. In some cities and regions, the full span of dates — October 28 to November 3 — is not widely known or celebrated.

Significance of Each Day

October 28 – The first candle is lit, and a white flower is placed on the altar for the souls of those who died suddenly, or through accidental or violent death.

October 29 – Honors the souls of those who drowned.

October 30 – A day to rememberx the lonely souls — those who were forgotten or homeless.

October 31 – At midnight, the gates of heaven open, allowing the spirits of unborn children to visit their families for 24 hours.

November 1 – Known as *Día de los Inocentes* (Day of the Innocents) or *Día de los Angelitos* (Day of the Little Angels), this day honors deceased children. Families spend the day at their graves, creating altars decorated with favorite foods, drinks, toys, and games. It is a deeply emotional and loving way to remember young lives lost.

November 2 – Known as *Día de los Fieles Difuntos* (Day of the Faithful Dead), this day is dedicated to honoring adult loved ones who have passed away.

November 3 – A day for bidding farewell. Families light the final candle and say goodbye to the lingering spirits, allowing them to return to the beyond until next year. This marks the closing of the Day of the Dead observances.

Biblical Reflections on Death and Remembrance

The Bible contains many verses that reflect on death and remembrance. Here are just a few that connect to the spirit of Day of the Dead:

Ecclesiastes 7:1
"A good name is better than precious oil; and the
day of death, than the day of one's birth."

Isaiah 25:8
"He will swallow up death forever; and the Lord
God will wipe away tears from all faces."

Job 14:5
"Man's days are determined; You (God) have decreed the
number of his months and have set limits he cannot exceed."

Ecclesiastes 9:5

"For the living know that they will die, but the dead know nothing...
Their love, their hatred, and their envy have now perished."

1 Thessalonians 4:14–18

This passage speaks of how "the dead in Christ will rise
first," and then those who are still alive will be "caught
up with them in the clouds to meet the Lord."

2 Corinthians 5:8

The apostle Paul reminds us that for believers, death is not
to be feared — it means being "at home with the Lord."

1 Corinthians 15

Describes how our spirits are only temporarily separated
from our bodies, and that one day, they will be reunited
with bodies that will never again die or decay.

A Time to Remember the Departed

Day of the Dead is a special time set aside to remember the departed for
seven days. The rest of the year belongs to the living, so it is only right that
we devote this time to honor those who have passed away.

Many cultures around the world celebrate their deceased loved ones
and ancestors. These celebrations range from lively and colorful festivals
to deeply spiritual gatherings. Although the details may differ, the meaning remains the same — to remember, honor, and celebrate those who
came before us.

Families often gather in cemeteries to honor their loved ones. They
bring flowers, candles, and offerings, tell stories, and play music. Even
with universal themes of remembrance, each country has its own customs and traditions for celebrating the lives of those who have passed.

Day of the Dead is not meant to be a sad time. It is a joyful celebration of life and memory — a way to give thanks for what our ancestors and loved ones gave us. While death may bring sorrow, this time is about welcoming the spirits back into our world, even if only for a moment.

In many ways, Day of the Dead is like a family reunion — except the guests of honor are the dead. It's a time to smile, laugh, and remember, knowing that our loved ones are with us in spirit.

Cemetery Visits and Home Altars

When families visit cemeteries during Day of the Dead, they spend the day with their loved ones who have passed. They clean and decorate the graves, place fresh flowers and candles, and sometimes even bring music. They share stories, memories, and laughter — believing the spirits are listening and smiling with them.

In many homes, altars are created as a way to remember the dead. These altars, or *ofrendas*, are decorated with photos, food, drinks, and items that were meaningful to the departed. This tells the spirits they are not forgotten. Families believe that the dead can hear their prayers, feel their love, and enjoy being remembered.

The Four Elements of Nature

In 450 BC, the ancient Greeks believed that four natural elements were connected to honoring the dead. These elements — fire, water, earth, and wind — are still symbolically represented during Day of the Dead.

- Fire – Represented by candle flames, which help guide the spirits on their journey.

- Water – Offered to quench the thirst of the spirits after their long travel.

- Earth – Represented by food placed at gravesites or altars, shared by both the living and the dead.

- Wind – Symbolized by *papel picado*, or cut paper banners, which flutter in the air and show the presence of spirit through movement.

Different Names, Shared Meaning

Around the world, many countries observe a version of Day of the Dead — sometimes under different names, but always with the same purpose: to remember and honor the deceased. Whether people are visiting cemeteries, lighting candles, or holding festivals, the heart of the tradition remains the same.

Here are some of the many names for this observance across cultures:

Día de los Muertos, Day of Ancestors, Day of Egun, All Souls Day, El Día de las Almas, Merelotz, All Souls Week, Jankanoo, Muharram, National Mourning Day, El Día de los Finados, Voodoo Festival, Ancestor Day, Qing Ming Festival, Día de los Santos Difuntos, Indigenous Festival, Svi Svete, Dušičky, Wag Festival, Tezkar, Hingedepäev, Allhallowtide, La Jour des Morts, La Fête des Morts, Giorgi Lomsadze.

Each of these reflects a cultural way of keeping the memory of the departed alive.

Celebrated Around the World

Many countries have their own ways of honoring the dead. Though the names and customs differ, the intention — to remember and celebrate those who have passed — connects people across continents and generations.

I've included a list of countries from around the world that celebrate Day of the Dead in their own way. Each place has its own customs, traditions, and names for honoring the dead — but they all share the same heartfelt purpose: to remember and celebrate those who have passed.

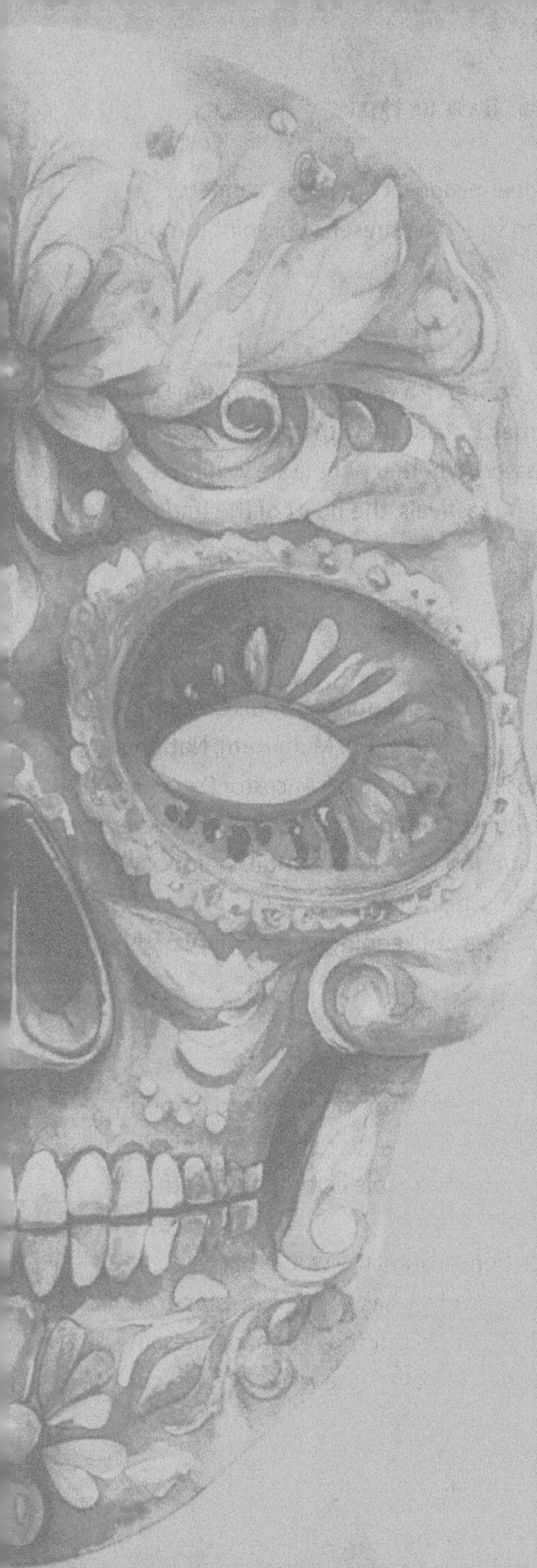

Albania

Vajtim or Gjemë

IN ALBANIA, *VAJTIM* OR *GJEMË* IS THEIR WAY OF HONORING THE DEATH OF a family member. Families may place the deceased in a sitting position on a chair so loved ones can see them and say their goodbyes. A eulogy is delivered by a family member. The burial usually happens on the same day, or shortly after the time of death. A wooden cross is placed on the grave to protect the deceased from vampires.

After the burial, families participate in a hand-washing ceremony before returning home. This ritual is believed to keep the spirit of the dead from following them. Remembrance ceremonies continue. Families gather again 7 to 9 days after the death, then on the 40th day, and once more between 6 months to a year later.

Andorra

All Souls' Day

IN THE COUNTRY OF ANDORRA, ALL SOULS' DAY IS CELEBRATED ON November 1st to honor deceased family members. The day begins at church and continues at the cemetery, where families decorate graves with flowers and light candles. These actions are meant to bring peace to the souls of the departed.

On this day, schools and businesses are closed, giving families time to be with their loved ones who have passed. Spending the day at the cemetery helps ease the sorrow of loss and strengthens the bond with ancestors.

Angola

Dia de Finados

IN ANGOLA, THE DAY OF THE DEAD IS KNOWN AS DIA DE FINADOS (ALL Souls Day) and is observed on November 2nd. Families attend church and visit cemeteries to pray for the souls of the departed. This tradition dates back to the 11th century and follows All Saints' Day. To this day, it remains a deeply meaningful observance.

During church services, the names of the deceased are read aloud, and prayers are offered for each one. At the cemetery, families clean the graves, lay flowers, and pray together. Afterward, they often gather at the home of the deceased to share a meal and honor their memory.

As part of the tradition, acts of charity are performed to help others — this is believed to aid the souls of the departed on their spiritual journey. The day is both a time of reflection and remembrance.

Antigua and Barbuda

Nine Night

IN ANTIGUA AND BARBUDA, THE FUNERAL TRADITION IS CALLED NINE Night. The celebration for the deceased begins on the ninth night. Families gather at the cemetery, placing flowers, food, and lighting candles to help the spirit find its way to the afterlife.

At night, the families hold a wake called "Dead Bones", which continues for nine days and ends on the final night. Then, the family hosts a party for the deceased, setting a table with the foods their loved one enjoyed in life.

On Nine Night, Antiguans and Barbudans believe that the spirit of the deceased appears in the doorway, passing through the party to say goodbye to their family. The spirit must walk through the door to enter the afterlife. A family member sees the spirit, then tells another person, and the message is passed along until the family collectively tells the deceased they may leave. After the spirit is gone, the family cannot eat until midnight.

Argentina

El Día de las Almas

IN ARGENTINA, THERE ARE DEEP TRADITIONS FOR HONORING THE DEAD through the celebration of El Día de las Almas (The Day of Souls). Families create ofrendas (offerings) at home and at the cemetery, placing favorite foods, drinks, *pan de muertos*, flowers, and candles for their loved ones.

November 1st is *Día de Todos los Santos* (All Saints' Day), also called Día de los Angelitos (Little Angels). November 2nd is dedicated to honoring adults. It is believed that on these days, the spirits return to the earth where they once lived. Families prepare for their arrival with food and prayers.

On November 1st and 2nd, family and friends gather at the cemetery to visit their loved ones, bringing food and flowers. Any leftover food is shared with others as an act of kindness.

In Argentina and other Spanish-speaking countries, the following words are commonly used when remembering the dead:

- ***La Muerte*** – the dead
- ***El Difunto*** – the deceased
- ***El Cadáver*** – the corpse
- ***El Velorio*** – the wake
- ***El Entierro*** – the burial

Armenia

Merelots

IN ARMENIA, MERELOTS IS THEIR DAY OF THE DEAD, OBSERVED BY THE Armenian Apostolic Church. It is celebrated on various days: the Monday after Christmas, Easter, the Feast of the Transfiguration, the Assumption of the Holy Virgin Mary, and the Exaltation of the Holy Cross.

Armenian funeral traditions have deep roots in ancient beliefs about death and the afterlife. It is said that on the last day of a person's life, an angel takes their final breath. At the cemetery, family and friends visit their loved ones. Priests pray for the departed, offer the Divine Liturgy, and perform a Requiem Mass, calling for kindness among all.

The traditional Armenian funeral takes place three days after death. The body remains at home, and the wake takes place there. The lid of the coffin is placed at the front door to signal that someone has passed. There are additional ceremonies held on the day of death, the funeral day, the day after the funeral, the 7th day, the 40th day, and on the one-year anniversary. On each of these days, families and friends gather for a meal and remember the life of their loved one.

Australia – Aboriginal

Sorry Business

AMONG ABORIGINAL AUSTRALIANS, DEATH IS PART OF A tradition known as "Sorry Business." This practice has two purposes: sending the spirit of the deceased to the next world and allowing the family and community to grieve.

Aboriginal people believe that life is just one part of a long spiritual journey. When a person dies, their spirit leaves the body and either returns to the ancestors or may linger and disturb the family. To support the spirit's journey, the name of the deceased is often avoided after death, as saying it may hold the spirit back.

During Sorry Business, families paint their bodies, sing, dance, and tell stories about the person who died. Burial sites are sacred and are remembered with stones, by carvings names on trees, or special markers to honor the person's life and memory.

Austria

Allerheiligen and Allerseelen

OR FAMILIES IN AUSTRIA, NOVEMBER 1ST IS KNOWN AS Allerheiligen (All Saints' Day), and November 2nd as *Allerseelen* (All Souls' Day). A special Requiem Mass is held in church to pray for the deceased. Families and friends gather to light candles, place chrysanthemums, marigolds, or wreaths on graves, and offer prayers for their loved ones. It's also a time of reunion for extended family members who may not have seen each other in years.

On *Allerheiligen*, Godparents give a sweet, braided yeast bread called *Allerheiligenstriezel* to their godchildren. *Allerseelen*, though not always a public holiday, remains a sacred day where families continue to honor the dead with visits to cemeteries and reflective prayer.

Azerbaijan

Death Anniversary / Ehsan Tradition

IN AZERBAIJAN, THE DECEASED ARE REMEMBERED ON SEVERAL KEY DAYS, including a special death anniversary observed during the second day of *Nowruz* (the Persian New Year). Families visit cemeteries to place flowers on the graves of relatives before celebrating the new year.

When a person dies in Azerbaijan, the body is laid facing south, covered with a black cloth, and a mirror is placed on the chest. It's believed the mirror reflects the soul and prevents the spirit from returning to disturb the living.

Regardless of wealth, every person is honored with a wake ceremony called *Ehsan* (which means "to do beautiful things"). Family and community members are served food as a form of blessing. It is customary for a female relative to prepare halva, and it is not polite to decline it. Friends and family gather again on the 3rd, 7th, and 49th days after death to offer prayers and remember the deceased.

BAHAMAS

Junkanoo

IN THE BAHAMAS, *JUNKANOO* IS A LIVELY CULTURAL FESTIVAL HELD ON December 26th (Boxing Day) and January 1st. It originated during slavery, when Africans were given a brief time off to celebrate. While *Junkanoo* is not a direct Day of the Dead, it is a powerful expression of heritage, joy, and spiritual connection.

Some traditions link *Junkanoo* to honoring ancestors. In some communities, funeral processions would pass through the streets with storytelling, music, and even talking to the dead. The celebration helps mark closure and a new beginning.

Due to limited burial space on the islands and the limestone terrain, graves are often reused, and decomposition typically occurs over about a decade. Most graves feature only a name and a simple cross.

BARBADOS

Day of the Ancestors / Day of the Egun

IN BARBADOS, THE DAY OF THE ANCESTORS OR *DAY OF THE EGUN* (A Yoruba word meaning "ancestors") is a time to celebrate the life of the departed. This tradition, rooted in African customs, includes food, music, storytelling, and the belief that the spirit of the deceased passes through the home during the wake.

The wake is called *Nine Night*, a significant event that begins on the first night after death. Family members stay awake to keep the spirit company, offering food like rice, dried meats, bread buns, cocoa, ginger, coffee, and alcohol throughout the night.

The second night is often called "Nancy Night" or "Anansi Story Night," when tales of the deceased are shared. On the third night, it is believed that the spirit reaches the afterlife, and the community gathers in honor.

BELARUS

Dziady and Radunitsa

IN BELARUS, ANCESTRAL REMEMBRANCE IS OBSERVED THROUGH TWO major traditions: *Dziady* and *Radunitsa*.

Dziady is a Slavic holiday to honor the spirits of ancestors, observed in autumn (October 31 to November 1). Families visit graves, light candles, leave food, and sometimes invite spirits into the home to share a symbolic meal. This tradition has pre-Christian, pagan roots and connects deeply with All Saints' Day.

Radunitsa is a springtime ritual held on the ninth day after Orthodox Easter. Families gather at cemeteries, clean graves, and hold outdoor meals to remember the dead. This week is called "Parental Week," emphasizing the role of family and community in honoring the departed.

Belgium

Toussaint / Allerheiligen

IN THE COUNTRY OF BELGIUM, *TOUSSAINT* (FRENCH) AND *ALLERHEILIGEN* (German) are both names for All Saints' Day, celebrated on November 1st. Both terms refer to the Catholic holiday recognizing all saints. The following day, November 2nd, is All Souls' Day, a day to remember the dead.

On All Saints' Day, families and friends visit cemeteries to decorate the graves of their loved ones with colorful chrysanthemum flowers and candles. On All Souls' Day, people gather at church and visit the graves again, saying prayers and giving thanks for the lives of those who have passed.

The origins of All Saints' Day date back to May 13, 609, when Pope Boniface IV accepted the Pantheon in Rome from Byzantine Emperor Phocas. On that same day, they honored the Blessed Virgin Mary. Later, in the year 835, Pope Gregory IV moved the celebration to November 1st.

BELIZE

Día de los Muertos / Día de los Finados

I**N THE COUNTRY OF BELIZE, THERE ARE SEVERAL TRADITIONS TO HONOR** the deceased. *Día de los Muertos*, or *Día de los Finados*, is observed on November 1st and 2nd. November 1st is dedicated to children, known as *Angelitos* (*Little Angels*), and November 2nd is for honoring adults.

After church, families visit the graves of their loved ones, saying prayers and placing marigold flowers (*cempazúchitl*), wreaths, and food offerings to share with the spirits. At home, families build altars (*ofrendas*) with the deceased's favorite foods.

In Belize, the Maya people also celebrate *El Día de los Finados*, a celebration of life after death. They believe in *Hanal Pixán* or *U Janal Pixano'ob*, meaning "food for the souls." This day is not about mourning but celebrating the eternal connection between life and death. Candles are lit to guide spirits back home, and food is placed to nourish the souls of the departed.

Bolivia

Día de los Muertos

IN BOLIVIA, THE CELEBRATION BEGINS ON NOVEMBER 1ST, CALLED *DÍA de los Angelitos* (*Little Angels*), and continues on November 2nd to honor adults. Cemeteries across Bolivia are filled with families decorating the graves of their loved ones.

Bolivian culture reflects a blend of Indigenous traditions and Spanish influences brought in the 15th and 16th centuries. At home, families create *ofrendas* (altars) and place the favorite foods of the deceased, such as candied pumpkin, *Pan de Muertos*, and drinks.

Breads shaped like angels, bulls, and ladders (to help the soul climb to heaven), along with *atole* and other traditional foods, are offered. Some families even place pillows and blankets so the spirits can rest.

On October 31st, many homes prepare a table with the deceased's favorite food so they can enjoy it when they return. Families also create colorful skulls, decorating them and asking for blessings such as health or protection. Parades, music, and dancing follow, turning mourning into joyful remembrance.

BRAZIL

Día de Finados

IN BRAZIL, *DÍA DE FINADOS* IS CELEBRATED ON NOVEMBER 2ND, A NATIONAL holiday to honor the dead. The first day, November 1st, is dedicated to children — called *Día de los Angelitos* (*Little Angels*) — while November 2nd is for adults.

After church services, families visit cemeteries to be with their loved ones, praying, remembering, and honoring their lives. At home, they build altars or *ofrendas* decorated with photos, sugar skulls, marigolds, favorite foods, and drinks so that the spirits can join their families for the day.

At the cemetery, families leave gifts, such as food and drinks, and decorate graves with wildflowers, daisies, chrysanthemums, gerberas, and candles to guide the souls on their journey.

Families often stay the entire day at the cemetery, sharing stories and *Pan de Muertos*, a sweet bread shaped like crossed bones. At night, Brazilians gather for parades and large celebrations to honor the spirits on this special day.

BULGARIA

Zadushnitsa

IN BULGARIA, *ZADUSHNITSA* IS OBSERVED AS A DAY OF THE DEAD OR ALL Souls' Day. It takes place on Saturdays before Lent, Pentecost, and the Feast of Archangel Michael, and it is meant to remember and pray for deceased family members.

At cemeteries, families clean the graves, light candles, pour wine on the grave in the shape of a cross, and bring food such as boiled wheat, candies, pastries, and bread rolls. These are offered to the dead and to other families visiting their loved ones. People say, "For God's forgiveness," and others respond, "May God forgive." Bulgarians believe that food nourishes the souls of the dead.

Clergy scatter wheat on graves, symbolizing rebirth in the spring, while boiled wheat reminds the living to care for their souls. Families also visit the graves on the 3rd, 9th, 20th, and 40th day after death, and later on the 3rd, 6th, 9th month, and one-year anniversaries.

CAMBODIA

Pchum Ben

FOR CAMBODIANS, *PCHUM BEN* IS THEIR DAY OF THE DEAD celebration. It lasts for 15 days and usually falls in September or October. It is Cambodia's second most important religious holiday after New Year's and is focused on honoring ancestors and the dead.

Families and communities pay respect to their ancestors in a practice rooted in centuries-old traditions of "benevolent giving." Food offerings — such as rice balls, sticky rice, coconut cream, and sesame seeds — are made for the spirits, who are believed to only eat during *Pchum Ben*. Some people throw rice into the air to feed wandering spirits.

To reduce bad karma, families pray and meditate at *pagodas* (Buddhist temples) and bring food for the monks and the spirits of their loved ones. Monks chant in *Pali* to transfer merit to the dead. Families also cook for monks and prepare food for hungry ghosts, who are not allowed to eat food meant for monks.

It is believed that bodies must not be dissected, as that could interfere with one's rebirth. Cambodians have three days off work during *Pchum Ben* to travel and reunite with their families.

CAMEROON

Crying the Death

IN CAMEROON, FUNERAL TRADITIONS DEPEND ON THE LIFE AND STATUS of the deceased. If the person had no children, mourning is not customary. If the deceased had children, the funeral becomes a significant ceremony, often lasting four to five hours.

The oldest family member is responsible for organizing the funeral. A second, more elaborate ceremony is held 40 days later, and families prepare food for guests who travel to the home of the deceased. Elders are considered especially important and are often given more elaborate burials.

The wake, known as the Nine Night, brings families together at home. They share food such as fish, pork, chicken, banana wraps, steamed plantains, and yams, while singing hymns and sharing memories of the deceased. During mourning, families wear special red and white clothing. At the end of the funerals, it is believed the deceased joins their ancestors.

CANADA

All Souls' Day

IN CANADA, *ALL SOULS' DAY* IS CELEBRATED ON NOVEMBER 2ND, AND *ALL Saints' Day* is observed on November 1st. On both days, families of the deceased visit cemeteries to decorate graves with flowers and light candles, offering prayers for the souls of their loved ones.

At church, families pray for the souls of the dead, and are invited to write names in a book known as the "Book of the Dead." Priests wear vestments in different colors to symbolize mourning, penance, and hope.

At home, Canadians often display photos and share stories of the deceased. Some prepare their loved ones' favorite meals and even bring the food to the cemetery, believing the deceased can smell the offerings. In some homes, families build altars (*ofrendas*) decorated with candles, marigolds, photos, and food.

Chile

Día de los Muertos

For Chileans, *DÍA DE LOS MUERTOS* IS CELEBRATED ON NOVEMBER 1st, known as *Día de los Angelitos* (*Little Angels*), and on November 2nd to honor adults. In some regions, people also celebrate on November 6th, depending on local customs.

After the death of a family member, a ritual called *Coflar* is held, where families sing and pray day and night for the deceased. There is also a tradition known as Yatiri Cleaning, where the clothes of the deceased are washed on the same day as the death.

In the homes of the deceased, altars (*ofrendas*) are built with pictures and offerings. Typical foods include *pozole*, *calabaza en tacha* (candied pumpkin with *piloncillo* and cinnamon), *flan*, and *atole*, a non-alcoholic corn-based drink that the deceased enjoyed.

At the cemetery, families bring gifts, sugar skulls, food, and candles. *Pan de Muertos* is shared with friends and family, music is played, and candles are lit to guide the souls to the afterlife. To honor their loved ones, people wear costumes, place *calaveras* and *cempazúchil* (marigold flowers), and dance to celebrate the life of the deceased. On the first anniversary, a special mass is held to honor the memory of the departed.

Note: In Chile, *Día de los Muertos* is celebrated more in Indigenous communities like the Aymara. Rituals like *Coflar* and *Yatiri* are Aymara traditions. Foods like *pozole* and *Pan de Muertos* are from Mexico but are sometimes included today.

CHINA

Qingming Festival

IN CHINA, THE *QINGMING FESTIVAL* IS COMPARABLE TO ALL SOULS' DAY. It is celebrated on April 4th or 5th, shortly after the spring equinox. *Qingming* means "pure brightness" and is rooted in Confucian traditions, with influences from Daoism, Buddhism, and Shenism. The festival has been observed for over 2,500 years and is a public holiday in China.

Families visit cemeteries to clean and decorate graves, making offerings of fruit, flowers, incense, and paper money. People burn incense, light candles, fly kites, and sometimes stage performances. *Willow branches* are also placed on graves or gates to ward off evil spirits.

A traditional food served is *Qingtuan* — a green dumpling made of glutinous rice and Chinese mugwort or barley grass.

COLOMBIA

Día de los Muertos

FOR COLOMBIANS, *DÍA DE LOS MUERTOS* IS CELEBRATED ON NOVEMBER 1st and 2nd. The first day, *Día de los Angelitos* (*Little Angels*), honors deceased children, and the second is dedicated to adults. This celebration blends Indigenous practices and Catholic traditions, symbolizing a reunion between the living and the dead.

In their homes, families build altars (*ofrendas*) decorated with food, drinks, photos, and *cempazúchil* flowers. These include the four elements: water, wind, earth, and fire, which are believed to nourish and guide the souls.

After attending church, families and friends go to the cemetery, bringing food and water for the deceased. Graves are decorated with candles and marigold flowers. In some towns, there is a parade with a symbolic casket carried through the village, ending at the cemetery.

Families also make sugar skulls, share *Pan de Muertos*, and write *calaveras literarias* — poetic verses dedicated to both the dead and the living.

Note: In Colombia, these traditions are more common in Indigenous and rural communities. Some customs like *Pan de Muertos*, *calaveras*, and *cempazúchil* come from Mexico, but are now shared through culture and celebration.

Costa Rica

Día de los Muertos / Día de Todos Santos / Día de Todos Almas

IN COSTA RICA, *DÍA DE LOS MUERTOS* IS ALSO CALLED *DÍA DE TODOS SANTOS* (All Saints' Day) and *Día de Todos Almas* (All Souls' Day). November 1st is for children (*Día de los Angelitos*), and November 2nd is for adults.

On November 2nd, families visit cemeteries, clean the graves, place flowers, and light candles to guide the souls. Traditional foods include *Pan de Muertos* and *Empanadas de Camote* (sweet potato turnovers). Food is shared among visitors and left for the dead.

Costa Ricans see this day as joyful rather than sad, choosing to celebrate life over mourning. In San José and other cities, families decorate graves of those without relatives, showing communal care. At home, they build altars (*ofrendas*) with candles, incense, food, and drink.

One of the most colorful traditions involves parades with large masquerade figures, including "Gigantes" (giants), witches, devils, and skulls. These characters are part of a masquerade tradition that began in the Central Valley during the colonial era, particularly in Cartago, where the Virgin of Los Angeles is honored each August.

CROATIA

Svi sveti

IN THE COUNTRY OF CROATIA, *SVI SVETI* IS THEIR NAME FOR ALL SAINTS' Day, celebrated on November 1st. It is also called *Dan svih svetih*, *Sisvete*, or *Sesvete*. Across the country, families visit cemeteries to honor the saints and loved ones who have passed.

At the graves, families light candles and place flowers — the most common being yellow and white chrysanthemums, called *krizanteme*. It's not a day of mourning, but a celebration of life and the good memories shared with those who are gone.

The tradition of honoring the dead has roots in different churches going back to the 4th century, first recorded in Antioch after Pentecost and mentioned in the writings of St. John Chrysostom. The Catholic Church later expanded the observance when King Louis made a proclamation in 835, allowed by Pope Gregory IV, turning it into a widespread *Communion feast*.

Today on *Svi sveti*, families all over Croatia visit cemeteries, leave flowers, and burn lanterns. The largest gathering is at Mirogoj Cemetery in Zagreb.

CUBA

Día de los Muertos

FOR CUBANS, *DÍA DE LOS MUERTOS* IS CELEBRATED ON NOVEMBER 1ST and 2nd. It was once celebrated in August, but later aligned with Western Christian observances: *All Saints' Eve* on October 31, *All Saints' Day* on November 1, and *All Souls' Day* on November 2.

This celebration dates back 2,500 to 3,000 years to pre-Columbian times, when Indigenous communities in Cuba honored the dead. Today, in Cuban homes, altars (*ofrendas*) are built to welcome back loved ones. These include photos, candles, favorite foods and drinks, and marigolds.

Families visit the graves, spending the day with their deceased loved ones. They share picnic meals, *Pan de Muertos*, sugar skulls, and corn-based drinks. Some wear skull masks or paint their faces, telling stories with smiles. It's a celebration that blends African, Indigenous, and Judeo-Christian beliefs — including readings from the Book of Ifá, the Torah, the Bible, and the Popol Vuh.

For Cubans, this day is not about sadness but about awakening the spirits and celebrating their lives.

Czech Republic

Dušičky

IN THE CZECH REPUBLIC, *DUŠIČKY* IS THEIR NAME FOR THE DAY OF THE DEAD, celebrated on November 2nd. The name comes from *duše*, meaning "soul." Other names for the day include *Památka zesnulých* (*Memorial of the Departed*) and *Vzpomínka na všechny věrné zesnulé* (*Remembrance of All the Faithful Departed*).

The holiday has roots in Roman Catholicism, but it is celebrated by both religious and non-religious people. After church, families go to the cemetery to decorate graves with flowers and candles.

Flowers represent the belief in eternal life, and candles symbolize resurrection and remembrance. Children's toys are placed on the graves of lost young ones, so their souls can play. Families also pray for the souls of the dead, especially for those in purgatory, and use the day to reflect.

Denmark

Døde Danskeres Dag

IN DENMARK, *DØDE DANSKERES DAG* MEANS DAY OF THE DEAD FOR DANES. When a loved one passes, a window is opened so their soul can leave, and candles are placed in the window to honor and remember them.

Funerals are usually held eight days after the death, either at a funeral home or church. Families read poems or deliver speeches, sing hymns, and a priest gives the eulogy at the service.

Danish funerals are about remembering life, sharing memories, good times, and laughter as families come together to say goodbye.

Note: Although Denmark doesn't have an official "Day of the Dead," personal and family rituals like candles in windows and storytelling at funerals are practiced.

Commonwealth of Dominica

All Saints' Day

ON CHRISTOPHER COLUMBUS'S SECOND VOYAGE, HE SIGHTED THE island of Dominica on November 3, 1493. Because it was a Sunday, he named it *Dies Dominica*, meaning "The Lord's Day" or "Sunday" in Latin.

The Carib Indians had inhabited the island for over six hundred years, and the Amerindians (Indigenous people of the Americas) had been there for more than three thousand years. The original name of the island was *Waitukubuli*, meaning "Tall is her body." For two centuries, this name was not officially recorded.

With the arrival of Christian traditions, death and burial practices changed — families no longer buried the deceased in the fetal position, as was once customary.

On *All Saints' Day*, families visit cemeteries and light candles on the graves of their loved ones. Cremation is not practiced in Dominica; all deceased are buried in cemeteries.

Dominican Republic

Día de los Muertos

IN THE DOMINICAN REPUBLIC, *DÍA DE LOS MUERTOS* IS OBSERVED ON November 1st and 2nd. On both days, families honor and remember the deceased with colorful altars, parades, and other community events.

Among the upper class, the viewing and visitation often take place in a funeral home, while poorer families hold the viewing in their home — known as being "laid out" for one day. The wake lasts through the night, expressing grief and love.

Families build altars (*ofrendas*) with photos, food, and personal belongings of the deceased. At the cemetery, they bring gifts, *calaveras*, and *cempazúchil* flowers, saying prayers throughout the day. *Pan de Muertos* is shared with friends and family. It's a day for the living to visit — but the dead are the guests of honor.

East Timor (Timor-Leste)

Day of the Dead

IN EAST TIMOR, DAY OF THE DEAD TRADITIONS GO BACK TO ANCIENT Indigenous civilizations. Families organize ceremonies and gatherings to help guide the deceased into their next life.

A two-week funeral ritual called *haha metan* ("black words") is observed. During this time, family and friends bring food and gifts, mourning with the family. It is believed that the deceased will return at night, and they are never forgotten.

Horses were used to carry the dead to the cemetery — a symbol of status and honor. Sometimes the horse was sacrificed to accompany the deceased into the afterlife.

At the cemetery, families pray, sing hymns, place flowers, and light candles, remembering their ancestors and celebrating their memory.

ECUADOR

Día de los Difuntos

IN ECUADOR, *DÍA DE LOS DIFUNTOS* IS CELEBRATED ON NOVEMBER 1ST AS *Día de los Angelitos* (*Little Angels*) and on November 2nd for adults. The holiday blends Catholic tradition and Indigenous rituals.

After church, families visit cemeteries to decorate graves with flowers, and they bring food to share with the dead. Traditional foods include *Guagua de Pan* (a sweet bread shaped like a doll or baby) and *colada morada* (a thick, purple fruit drink made with blue or black corn flour, berries, and spices).

At home, altars are created with photos, fruit, bread, water, salt, incense, and candles. Days before the holiday, families gather to clean the graves of multiple relatives often buried together.

In recognition of its cultural importance, *Día de los Difuntos* was declared an Intangible Cultural Heritage of Humanity by UNESCO.

EGYPT

Wag Festival

IN EGYPT, THE *WAG FESTIVAL* IS THEIR ANCIENT DAY OF THE DEAD, celebrated in August, during the month of *Thout* in the Coptic calendar. The festival is dedicated to Osiris, the God of the Dead, the afterlife, and resurrection.

To honor the deceased and remember the death of Osiris, families place small boats in rivers, symbolizing the soul's journey to the afterlife. Ancient Egyptians believed in the underworld, called *Duat*, which could only be reached by traveling through tombs. This realm was home to gods, demons, souls, and figures like Osiris, Anubis, Thoth, Horus, Hathor, and Maat.

To guide the soul, priests performed rituals, including purification, anointing, chanting, and reciting spells. Ceremonial artifacts were touched to the mummy, helping the deceased awaken their senses in the afterlife. The *Book of the Dead* offered spells and instructions, helping the soul speak sacred names and respond to the gods.

Today, families gather at cemeteries to pray, recite the Quran, and bring offerings of fruit, flowers, and palm leaves. There are also eight additional cemetery days, called *ziyaras*, once observed by lower-class Egyptians but no longer widely practiced.

El Salvador

El Día de los Difuntos

IN EL SALVADOR, *EL DÍA DE LOS DIFUNTOS* IS CELEBRATED ON NOVEMBER 1st for children, called *Día de los Angelitos* (*Little Angels*), and November 2nd for adults.

Families and friends visit cemeteries to clean and decorate graves, pray, and sing songs the deceased enjoyed. They believe that if you remember the dead, they remain part of your life. Though it brings connection, it can also bring back painful memories of loved ones lost.

The tradition has pre-colonial roots from the Aztec and Toltec civilizations, who believed that death is a natural part of life. Today, it blends Catholic rituals and Indigenous customs.

One of the highlights is *La Calabiuza*, celebrated in early November. During this event, people dress as skeletons, dance in the streets, and carry torches — a tradition tied to Indigenous heritage.

Equatorial Guinea

Día de los Muertos

IN EQUATORIAL GUINEA, *DÍA DE LOS MUERTOS* IS CELEBRATED ON November 1st and 2nd. After attending mass, families visit cemeteries to be with their departed loved ones, lighting candles and offering flowers and food.

They believe this is a time when God calls all souls toward sainthood, and families prepare by creating a path of flower petals and candles, guiding the deceased back home. Favorite foods are placed around the house, at shrines, or on tombs to welcome them.

On November 1st, a memorial mass is held at 9 a.m. in cemetery chapels. On November 2nd, families return to the graves with flowers, prayers, and shared meals in memory of the departed.

ESTONIA

Hingedepäev

IN ESTONIA, *HINGEDEPÄEV*, OR DAY OF THE DEAD, IS CELEBRATED ON November 2nd. From late autumn through year's end, Estonians observe what they call "Soul Time", when the living and the dead are believed to connect.

Foggy days signal that the dead are near. Families light candles, placing them on windowsills or at cemeteries to honor their ancestors. Homes are cleaned, and special meals are prepared to please the spirits and ensure good harvests and animal health.

In the evening, names of the deceased are spoken aloud, guiding spirits home. Laughing, loud noise, or joking is avoided out of respect — as spirits need quiet to rest until spring.

Birds are powerful soul symbols, and windy days mean the dead are restless. Food and drinks are placed out for visiting spirits, ensuring they feel welcome.

Finland

Kekri

IN FINLAND, THE DAY OF THE DEAD IS CALLED *KEKRI*, CELEBRATED FROM October 31st to November 2nd. It is a festival of the harvest and the ancestors, observed with music, dancing, and ceremonies at home.

Altars are built to honor the dead, and a plate is placed at the table for the spirits. The Finnish believe that every object, animal, and plant has its own spirit, or *tonttu*, which must be protected and respected.

In the past, people believed the dead could hear everything, so they spoke softly and only said kind things. Families welcomed spirits by pouring ale from the road to the door and lit bonfires and lanterns to keep evil spirits away. If the ancestors were pleased, they would protect the family and its land.

FRANCE

La Toussaint

IN FRANCE, *LA TOUSSAINT* — OR ALL SAINTS' DAY — IS A NATIONAL holiday celebrated on November 1st. The word *Toussaint* comes from *tous les saints*, meaning "all the saints," and the day is used to honor both known and unknown saints.

Families attend church mass, lighting candles for each departed loved one. Then, they visit cemeteries, bringing photos and flowers such as *chrysanthèmes* (chrysanthemums), *bruyère* (heather), and *couronnes d'immortelles* (everlasting wreaths). Some light candles to symbolize joy in the afterlife.

La Toussaint is considered a peaceful day, a time for families to gather and spend quiet moments remembering the dead.

GABON

All Saints' Day

IN GABON, *ALL SAINTS' DAY* ON NOVEMBER 1ST IS A SPECIAL TIME TO honor ancestors and celebrate memories. It is a day that strengthens the bond between the living and the dead.

Families visit cemeteries to clean and decorate graves, laying flower petals from the grave to the home to welcome the spirits. Because of the tropical climate, bodies are buried within two days in wooden coffins, after being rubbed to remove rigor mortis.

Later, through Bwiti ceremonies (a spiritual discipline), the deceased is welcomed into the ancestral world. A mourning ceremony called *de deuil* is held one year later to end the grieving period and honor the spirit's transition.

GEORGIA

Giorgi Lomsadze (Easter Monday Observance)

IN GEORGIA, THE DAY OF THE DEAD IS OBSERVED ON THE MONDAY AFTER Easter. On this day, families visit cemeteries to share food, wine, and memories with their loved ones who have passed.

The family appoints a *tamasa* (toastmaster) to speak on behalf of the dead, offering toasts and stories. Families bring red-painted eggs, a bottle of wine, and traditional foods like *khachapuri* (cheese bread), *blinchiki* (meat rolls), *sulguni* cheese, *jonjoli* (pickled greens), strawberries, and *paska* (Easter cake). They also bring homemade sweet grape juice.

It is tradition to pour wine on the grave so the deceased can "drink" with their family. For Georgians, life continues after death — and the dead are never forgotten.

GERMANY

Totensonntag / All Saints' Day / All Souls' Day

IN GERMANY, THE DAY OF THE DEAD IS OBSERVED THROUGH DIFFERENT traditions, including *Totensonntag* (Sunday of the Dead), *All Saints' Day*, and *All Souls' Day*.

Totensonntag (also called *Ewigkeitssonntag* or *Totenfest*) is a Protestant remembrance day, held on the last Sunday of the liturgical year. *All Saints' Day* on November 1st and *All Souls' Day* on November 2nd are Catholic celebrations where families visit graves, attend Mass, and light candles and incense.

One tradition is the *Leichenpredigt*, a funeral sermon popular since the 16th century, which includes a *vita* (life story) of the deceased. After the burial, families gather for a meal called *Leichenschmaus* (funeral feast), often including a sweet cake called *Zuckerkuchen*.

It is believed this meal is shared between the living and the dead.

Ghana

Funeral Celebrations

IN GHANA, FUNERALS ARE SEEN AS BOTH A CELEBRATION OF LIFE AND A tribute to the dead. Coffins are often custom-made in shapes that reflect the person's profession or personality — like a fish, a shoe, or a hammer.

Funerals can last for several days and often take place on Saturdays. They include dancing, food, drinks, and music, blending jazz and African rhythms. Talking drums are played — not just for rhythm, but to tell stories about the deceased's life and their journey to the afterlife.

Mourning traditions differ by gender: men mourn for three days, and women for four. After the funeral, families serve a meal of *fufu*, *tuo zafi*, *ampesi*, *jollof*, *banku*, meats, and alcoholic drinks.

The chiefs and elders sit under a large umbrella, overseeing the celebration. Ghanaians hold deep respect for their ancestors, who are believed to stay close and protect the living.

GRENADA

Day of the Dead

IN GRENADA, DAY OF THE DEAD IS CELEBRATED ON NOVEMBER 1ST AND 2nd as a time to remember and honor loved ones who have passed. It is believed that the spirits return to celebrate with their families.

Families bring food, drinks, and music to the graveyard, surrounded by the glow of candles throughout the night. At home, altars are built with photos, mementos, favorite foods, and drinks.

Decorations may include skeletons made of clay, wood, or papier-mâché, as well as *catrinas* and *catrines* in large, feathered hats or top hats. *papel picado* (cut paper banners) are also used.

At cemeteries, families sing, play music, dance, and share meals with the dead — keeping memories alive through joy and tradition.

Guatemala

Día de los Muertos

IN GUATEMALA, *DÍA DE LOS MUERTOS* IS CELEBRATED OVER SEVERAL DAYS, from October 31st to November 2nd. *Día de los Angelitos* (*Little Angels*) is on November 1st for children, and November 2nd is for adults. Guatemalans believe the spirits return to visit their families during this time.

One of Guatemala's most vibrant traditions is flying giant kites, called *barriletes*, some reaching up to five stories high. These colorful kites are sent from homes and cemeteries to guide the spirits home. At the end of the day, the kites are burned to let the spirits rest in peace.

At cemeteries, families gather with mariachi or marimba bands, bringing foods like spiced stews, tamales, and *fiambre* (a cold vegetable and meat salad). At home, altars (*ofrendas*) are built with the deceased's favorite food and drinks.

Día de los Muertos in Guatemala has been recognized by UNESCO as an Intangible Cultural Heritage of Humanity.

Equatorial Guinea

Day of the Dead

IN EQUATORIAL GUINEA, DAY OF THE DEAD IS OBSERVED ON NOVEMBER 1st and All Saints' Day on November 2nd. It is believed that the souls of the dead return to Earth during this time.

At home, families light candles and lay flower petals from the cemetery to their doors to guide the spirits home. They prepare the deceased's favorite foods, placing them around the house, shrine, or tomb so the spirits can enjoy a meal.

On November 1st at 9 a.m., a mass is held at the cemetery chapel. Families then visit the graves, clean them, and light candles and place flowers. It's a day of reunion and remembrance.

GUINEA-BISSAU

All Souls' Day

ON NOVEMBER 1, 1898, A PORTUGUESE OFFICER, HENRIQUE AUGUSTO Dias de Carvalho, witnessed the people of Guinea-Bissau celebrating *Día dos Finados* (*All Souls' Day*) in the streets. The celebration began at midnight on November 2nd.

Families gathered at church, holding small lights, then walked through the streets singing *Ave Maria* mixed with African songs. They wore vibrant costumes, dancing and drinking *aguardiente* (a strong distilled wine) for three days and nights.

On the final night, families sang again, asking for blessings for the souls of the dead. The celebration was joyful and loud, filled with movement, music, and prayer.

GUYANA

Día de los Muertos

IN GUYANA, *DÍA DE LOS MUERTOS* IS OBSERVED ON NOVEMBER 1ST FOR children (*Angelitos*), November 2nd for adults, and November 3rd to celebrate all lives.

In homes, altars (*ofrendas*) are decorated with photos, mementos, and favorite foods and drinks of the deceased. Some families also build altars at the cemetery.

Foods like Guyanese gumbo, codfish salad, and flan are prepared and placed on the altar for the spirits to smell and enjoy. It is a day to celebrate life, remember the dead, and exchange mourning for joy.

After the funeral comes the "nine night", a traditional wake ceremony held nine days later in memory of the deceased. Mirrors in the home are covered to avoid seeing the dead, and the house is swept to push the spirits away, so they don't take anyone with them.

Many customs are influenced by Christian practices, blended with local and African traditions.

HAITI

Fet Gede (Festival of the Dead)

OR THE PEOPLE OF HAITI, *FET GEDE*, OR THE FESTIVAL OF THE DEAD, IS their Day of the Dead. It takes place on November 1st and 2nd and blends Catholic traditions with Vodou and Gede rituals.

After attending church, families go to cemeteries to visit the dead, honoring their ancestors, asking for favors, or giving thanks to the spirits. At home, altars are built with photos, food, candles, and offerings.

Special drawings called *veves* (geometric symbols used in Vodou) are made to attract the spirits. Offerings are given with dancing, drumming, and rituals. In some ceremonies, goats are sacrificed, and their blood is smeared on the forehead and tongue of participants.

The *Gede* are Vodou spirits of death and fertility. They escort souls to the afterlife and often appear in ceremonies as joyful, trickster-like figures who keep the connection between the living and the dead alive.

Honduras

Día de los Muertos

IN HONDURAS, *DÍA DE LOS MUERTOS* IS CELEBRATED ON NOVEMBER 1ST for children (*Día de los Angelitos*) and November 2nd for adults. Families remember their loved ones in different ways depending on the region and tradition.

At home, families create altars (*ofrendas*) with photos, flowers, and the deceased's favorite food and drinks to encourage the soul to return and bless the living.

At cemeteries, graves are cleaned and decorated, and families spend time eating, praying, and remembering joyful moments. At night, candles are lit to guide spirits to the afterlife, and some families stay awake through the night to keep them company.

Hong Kong

Qingming (Tomb Sweeping Day)

I**N HONG KONG, THE *QINGMING FESTIVAL* — OR TOMB SWEEPING DAY —** is held 15 days after the spring equinox according to the Chinese lunisolar calendar, usually in early April, not November.

Families visit cemeteries to clean, sweep, and decorate the graves of ancestors. They burn incense, paper money, and make food offerings to honor the spirits. This practice dates back over 2,500 years to the Zhou Dynasty, when emperors performed ancestral sacrifices.

Funeral customs are symbolic, including funeral attire, where children and in-laws wear black, while others may wear lighter or festive colors. *Feng shui* masters (geomancers) help choose burial spots, and offerings continue for seven days after death and sometimes longer.

Hungary

Halottak Napja

IN HUNGARY, *HALOTTAK NAPJA*, OR DAY OF THE DEAD, IS OBSERVED ON November 1st. It is a national holiday where Hungarians honor their deceased loved ones.

Families visit cemeteries to clean graves or tombstones, and place flowers and candles to guide the dead to the spirit world. During the funeral, some throw dirt and handkerchiefs onto the grave to show sorrow, then walk around the grave several times.

After the funeral, families return home for a shared meal, setting a plate for the deceased that includes traditional dishes like paprikash, bread, and wine. These meals are about sharing memories and inviting the dead back home in spirit.

Originally a Catholic feast for martyred saints, *All Saints' Day* was set on November 1st by the eighth century and continues to be a public holiday in Hungary today.

ICELAND

Erfi (Funeral Feast and Remembrance)

IN ICELAND, THE DEAD ARE HONORED ON DECEMBER 24TH, WHEN FAMILIES visit graves and light candles. Funerals are conducted in churches by priests, after which the coffin is buried or cremated. A wooden cross, flowers, and a wreath are placed on the grave.

Erfi is an old Norse word for a funeral feast, a tradition that honors the deceased and brings family together. At home, altars are prepared with candles, water, food, and family photos to welcome the spirits back.

In ancient times, burial mounds called *haugur* were built as final resting places for chiefs, warriors, and nobles. Even today, Icelanders name their children after deceased relatives — a way to honor memory and keep the family line alive.

India

Shraddha

FAMILIES IN INDIA CELEBRATE *SHRADDHA* DURING PITRU PAKSHA, A 16-day observance held in September or October, depending on the lunar calendar. *Shraddha* is their Day of the Dead, where rituals are performed to honor ancestors and seek their blessings.

A key ritual is *Tarpan*, the offering of water as a symbol of nourishment and purification. On the first death anniversary, families hold a memorial service at home, which includes chanting, prayers, scripture readings, and a communal feast.

A traditional meal offering called *Pinda Daan* — rice balls made for spiritual nourishment — is offered to satisfy the hunger of the departed soul. Different tribes in India have their own cultural death rites. Some paint the face of the deceased red, others wash the body with yucca, and some tie feathers around the head as symbolic prayers — all done out of respect for the dead.

Note: Some tribal details like yucca washing and feather-tying, may reflect generalized or non-Indian customs. These practices are not widely documented within Indian tribal traditions.

Indonesia

Ma'nene

IN INDONESIA, THE *MA'NENE* RITUAL IS OBSERVED BY THE TORAJAN PEOPLE of Sulawesi as their form of Day of the Dead. Families exhume the bodies of their ancestors, clean and groom them, and dress them in new clothes. This practice serves as a way to reunite with loved ones and honor their memory.

Families often take photos with the bodies, treating them as part of the gathering. After the ceremony, the bodies are returned to their tombs, where they will remain until the next ritual, which is typically done every one to three years.

The *Ma'nene* festival begins in the morning and lasts through the afternoon. Once the corpses are redressed, they are ceremonially returned to their graves. It is believed that this ritual leads to better harvests and blessings in the following year.

Each region in Indonesia has its own cultural approach to death, reflecting a wide range of spiritual and philosophical beliefs.

IRAN

Frawardigan

IN IRAN, THE *FRAWARDIGAN* FESTIVAL HONORS THE SPIRITS OF THE dead during the last five days of the Zoroastrian year. It is a time to welcome ancestral spirits, offer prayers, and prepare for the New Year (Nowruz).

The *Amesha Spentas* — seven holy immortals in Zoroastrianism — are also honored. In the Sasanian Empire, the festival was divided into two parts: the *lesser panje*, for sinless souls and children, and the *greater panje*, for all souls.

Iranian funerals are conducted in multiple stages: the body is washed, wrapped in white cloth, and placed in a wooden coffin, then buried facing Mecca. Family and friends mourn on the 3rd, 7th, and 40th day after death, wearing black to symbolize grief.

Sherbet, a sweet drink, is served as a symbol of paradise, representing the joy of the soul in the afterlife. Families often hang cloth banners and photos of the deceased on the wall to honor them during mourning.

IRELAND

Samhain

IN IRELAND, *SAMHAIN* IS A THREE-DAY CELTIC FESTIVAL OF THE DEAD, celebrated from October 31st to November 2nd. It marked the end of the harvest and the beginning of the dark half of the year. The ancient Irish believed that during this time, the boundary between the living and the dead became thin.

In the 14th century, the Catholic Church established November 1st and 2nd as holy days of obligation, blending Christian teachings with the ancient feast of the dead. It was believed that souls in purgatory were released to roam the Earth, seeking prayers from the living.

Families built bonfires to ward off evil spirits, and left food offerings to invite the dead home for a meal. They visited graves to clean and decorate headstones, placing flowers and candles. At home, an empty plate was left on the table and windows or doors were left open to welcome spirits.

Superstitions on *All Souls' Night* included: ghosts seen in lonely places, shooting stars signaling a soul's ascent to heaven, and advice to stay indoors after dark so wandering souls wouldn't follow.

ISRAEL

Yahrzeit and Yizkor

IN ISRAEL, THERE IS NO DAY OF THE DEAD, BUT JEWISH TRADITION includes two important memorial observances: *Yahrzeit* and *Yizkor*. *Yahrzeit* comes from the Yiddish words *yahr* (year) and *tzeit* (time). It marks the anniversary of a person's death, according to the Hebrew calendar. On this day, families light a 24-hour memorial candle, called a *yizkor candle*, in the evening and recite the *Kaddish*, a special prayer honoring the deceased.

Yizkor, meaning "may God remember," is said four times a year during synagogue services: on Yom Kippur, Shemini Atzeret, the eighth day of Passover, and the second day of Shavuot. It is a communal prayer for remembering the dead.

Jewish mourning traditions include *Shiva* (the first seven days after burial) and *Shloshim* (thirty days of mourning). Families visit graves at any time, especially on fast days or before holy days, often placing a small stone with their left hand to signify remembrance.

On *Yahrzeit*, families are inspired by the memory of their loved one, doing good deeds, studying Torah, or using their gifts in meaningful ways to honor their legacy.

Italy

Giorno dei Morti

IN ITALY, *GIORNO DEI MORTI* — OR ALL SOULS' DAY — IS CELEBRATED ON November 2nd. In Sicily, it's called *Jornu di li Morti*, where it's believed that the dead return to visit their loved ones and leave gifts for children, much like Christmas morning.

Ognissanti (All Saints' Day) is observed on November 1st, followed by *Il Giorno dei Morti* on the 2nd. Families visit cemeteries with flowers and candles, leave sweets, wine, or water as offerings, and prepare traditional foods like:

Pane dei morti (bread of the dead)
Fave dei morti (fava bean cookies)
Ossi dei morti (bones of the dead)
Pupi ri zuccaru (sugar dolls representing the dead)

At home, a place is set at the table for the spirits, and children leave their shoes outside, hoping to receive treats. Some go door-to-door calling *"Morti! Morti!"* to collect sweets.

The celebration blends Catholic, Roman, and ancient pagan traditions, with connections to Samhain, the festival marking the end of the harvest and beginning of the spiritual season.

Note: Pagan links to Samhain are symbolic, not direct historical fact.

Jamaica

Nine Night

IN JAMAICA, THERE IS NO *DÍA DE LOS MUERTOS*, BUT THERE IS *NINE NIGHT* — a Caribbean funerary tradition that supports the family and honors the deceased nine days after death.

Family and friends gather at the deceased's home to share memories, sing hymns, eat, and play music. The gathering is influenced by African and European Christian beliefs.

Traditionally, it was believed that it took nine nights for the soul to return to Africa to find peace. On the ninth night, the family prepares a table with food and gifts to guide the spirit to its final resting place on the tenth day.

Nine Night is also called *Dead Yard*. Celebrants sing spiritual folk songs called *sankeys* and dance the *Dinki-Mini*, a traditional dance inviting the spirit to join.

On the final night, people eat goat or pork, drink white rum, and share stories — but no one eats until after midnight, marking the moment when the soul is believed to leave for the afterlife.

Japan

Obon (Bon Festival)

IN JAPAN, *OBON*, OR THE BON FESTIVAL, IS A MULTI-DAY BUDDHIST celebration held from August 13th to 15th, though some regions like Tokyo observe it in July. It is their version of the Day of the Dead, rooted in the Buddhist *Urabon-kyo* sutra.

The festival commemorates the spirits of ancestors, believed to return home during *Obon*. Families hang lanterns, prepare food offerings, and perform bon odori dances to send "good karma" to their ancestors. Taiko drums are often part of the festivities.

At temples and home altars, families offer fruit, incense, and flowers. Many set up two altars called *shōryō-dana* — one for ancestors, the other for wandering spirits.

One of the most beautiful traditions is the floating of paper lanterns (*tōrō nagashi*) down rivers or into the sea, symbolizing the spirits' return to the other world.

At funerals (*tsuya*), a Buddhist priest recites sutras (*kyō*) beside the deceased (*hotokesama*) before placing them in a *hitsugi* (coffin). Family and friends gather to share stories and pay respect.

Korea (North & South)

Chuseok

IN NORTH AND SOUTH KOREA, *CHUSEOK* IS A HARVEST AND ANCESTRAL holiday celebrated on the 15th day of the 8th month of the lunar calendar, around the full moon in early fall. This three-day celebration honors ancestors and family unity, a tradition observed long before the country was divided.

In South Korea, families travel to their hometowns to visit ancestral graves, clean the tombs, and offer food and drinks, including *songpyeon* (rice cakes), *sindoju*, and *dongdongju* (types of rice wine).

The arrangement of food on the table is symbolic:

North – rice and soup
South – fruits and vegetables
West – meats
East – rice cakes and drinks

In some regions, before burial, a shamanic ritual is performed to ward off evil spirits. In North Korea, *Chuseok* is less emphasized publicly, though some private ancestral practices continue.

Note: The food arrangement and shamanic rites are practiced
more commonly in South Korea. North Korea observes
fewer public rituals due to its political context.

Laos

Boun Khao Salak & Boun Ho Khao Padabdin

IN LAOS, THE DAY OF THE DEAD IS CELEBRATED THROUGH MULTIPLE Buddhist festivals, including *Boun Khao Salak*, observed on the 10th full moon of the lunar calendar, and *Boun Ho Khao Padabdin*, celebrated on the 14th or 15th day of the 9th lunar month.

During *Khaw Sahlaat*, families visit temples to offer food, fruit, candles, incense, and written lists of ancestors to monks. The belief is that the spirits of the dead are released from suffering, especially during *Boun Padabdin*, when spirits are said to roam the earth.

Offerings are made to show gratitude and respect to ancestors and guardian spirits. These ceremonies include prayers, chanting, and sometimes release of birds or symbolic items to represent freedom for the souls.

Note: These Lao festivals combine Theravada Buddhism
with animist traditions. *Padabdin* is especially known for
its ancestral focus. Timing varies slightly each year.

LATVIA

Mirušo piemiņas diena

IN LATVIA, *MIRUŠO PIEMIŅAS DIENA* IS THE DAY OF THE DEAD, OBSERVED on the last Sunday of November. It overlaps with *Svecīšu vakars* (Night of Candles), when families light candles at cemeteries across the country to honor their departed.

Other seasonal rituals include *Mikeļdiena*, the autumn solstice festival, and the beginning of *Veļu laiks* ("Time of the Dead"), when bread, cheese, butter, and other foods are offered to keep spirits at peace.

The cemetery festival *Kapu svētki* is another tradition where families gather for remembrance and community. In ancient times, Latvians buried the dead with bread, beer, and protective charms, and waved an axe to ward off *vēļi* (ghosts or phantoms).

At home, families clean the house, set a table, and invite the dead to visit. Death is seen as a natural part of life, with rituals to help both the living and the spirits find peace.

Note: *Veļu laiks*, *Svecīšu vakars*, and *Kapu svētki* are distinct Latvian traditions. Practices like waving an axe and inviting spirits home are part of folk beliefs.

LITHUANIA

Vėlinės or Ilgės

IN LITHUANIA, *VĖLINĖS* or *ILGĖS* IS THE DAY OF THE DEAD, OBSERVED ON November 2nd. It blends Christian and ancient pagan traditions, honoring the souls of the deceased.

Families visit cemeteries in large numbers, clean graves, decorate them with flowers, and light candles. The day before, many attend church services and prepare for All Souls' Day, believing that the souls of the dead return to visit during these two days.

Since the mid-19th century, Lithuanians have maintained the tradition of lighting grave candles to guide and comfort the spirits. *Vėlinės* is a deeply spiritual time of reflection, prayer, and respect.

LUXEMBOURG

Allerseelen / Allerhellegen

IN LUXEMBOURG, *ALLERHELLEGEN* (ALL SAINTS' DAY) IS CELEBRATED ON November 1st, and *Allerseelen* (All Souls' Day) on November 2nd. Originally celebrated together, these days now serve different purposes.

On *Allerhellegen*, families remember deceased loved ones, attend Mass, and visit cemeteries, placing flowers and candles. On *Allerseelen*, the focus shifts to souls in purgatory, and priests bless the graves.

A unique Luxembourgish tradition on the eve of All Saints' Day is *D'Trauliicht brennen* — where men carve scary faces into hollowed-out beets or turnips, light candles inside, and hang them outside churches or on streets. These lanterns protect the family from spirits and light the way into winter.

> Note: *D'Trauliicht brennen* is a distinct local tradition. Beets and turnips predate pumpkins in such lantern customs. Catholic observance of *Allerhellegen* and *Allerseelen* is national.

MADAGASCAR

Famadihana

IN MADAGASCAR, *FAMADIHANA*, OR THE "TURNING OF THE BONES," IS THE island's traditional Day of the Dead celebration. The ritual began in the 17th century, influenced by Southeast Asian and Oceanic customs.

Every five to seven years, families exhume the body from the tomb, clean the remains, and rewrap them in fresh cloth. This is a moment to reconnect with the dead, celebrate their life, and welcome them back into the world of the living and ancestors.

After dancing, music, and storytelling, the body is returned to the tomb. *Famadihana* is about kinship, a reminder of the unbreakable bond between the living, the dead, and their lineage.

Note: Famadihana is unique to the Merina people of Madagascar. It continues as a family-centered ritual, though less frequent due to modern challenges.

Malaysia

Qingming Festival / Ari Muyang

IN MALAYSIA, THE *QINGMING FESTIVAL*, ALSO KNOWN AS *ARI MUYANG* among Indigenous communities, is based on the lunar calendar and held in early April. It dates back to the Ming and Qing dynasties and blends Chinese and local traditions.

Families visit ancestral graves, clean the tombs, and offer flowers, incense, food, and fruit. *Ari Muyang* includes altars, traditional dancing, and rituals to honor and thank the dead for past blessings and ask for future prosperity.

The feast is shared at the tombs as a solemn family ritual and a reflection of love and gratitude. It is both a spiritual obligation and a celebration of ancestry.

Note: *Qingming* is widely practiced by Chinese Malaysians. *Ari Muyang* reflects Indigenous traditions; their observance varies by community.

MALTA

L-Għid tal-Erwieħ / L-Għid tal-Imwiet

IN MALTA, *L-GĦID TAL-ERWIEĦ* OR *L-GĦID TAL-IMWIET* IS OBSERVED ON November 2nd, known as All Souls' Day. November is called *ix-xahar tal-mejtin*, or the "Month of the Dead."

Families gather at cemeteries, decorating graves with flowers and candles to guide the souls to the afterlife. Traditions include lighting oil lamps for 40 days near a crucifix or an image of the Madonna, kneeling at graves, feeding the poor, and praising the virtues of the deceased.

This sacred day is about remembrance, charity, and reflection, deeply rooted in Catholic faith and Maltese cultural identity.

MAURITIUS

Mautourco / Ghoon Festival

IN MAURITIUS, *FÊTE DES MORTS* OR *ALL SOULS' DAY* IS CELEBRATED ON November 2nd, the day after *All Saints' Day*. Families attend church services, then visit cemeteries, clean graves, pray, and bring flowers.

It is also a family reunion, a moment when the dead are remembered, and their spirit welcomed from November 1st to 2nd.

Mauritian Shiite Muslims also observe the *Ghoon Festival*, a mourning ritual passed down through generations. It is marked by reflection, prayer, and the preparation of traditional foods — a blend of African, Chinese, Indian, and European influences.

Mexico

Día de los Muertos

IN MEXICO, *DÍA DE LOS MUERTOS* IS CELEBRATED FROM OCTOBER 31ST TO November 2nd. *Día de los Angelitos* ("Little Angels") is on November 1st for children, and November 2nd is for adults.

Families build altars (*ofrendas*) at home, decorated with the dead's favorite foods, flowers, candles, and photos. *Pan de Muertos* is prepared in various shapes, and guests are often welcomed to view the altars and share in *atole*, a warm corn-based drink.

People paint their faces as colorful skulls, and *calaveras* and *catrinas* symbolize the joyful acceptance of death as part of life.

Note: *Día de los Muertos* is a UNESCO-recognized celebration.

Moldova

Paștele Blajinilor

IN MOLDOVA, *PAȘTELE BLAJINILOR*, OR EASTER OF THE BLESSED ONES, IS celebrated two days after Orthodox Easter.

Families gather at cemeteries to clean graves, place flowers and candles, and offer wine, painted eggs, food, and candy. It is a joyful day, full of laughter, food-sharing, and remembrance.

A priest blesses each grave, followed by a choir singing hymns. Families share food with neighbors and give gifts to children, believing this honors the memory of their dead.

Myanmar

Prayer for the Spirits

IN MYANMAR, *PRAYER FOR THE SPIRITS* IS A NOVEMBER REMEMBRANCE ritual, honoring the souls of the dead. Families visit cemeteries, light candles, and sing songs. Religious leaders — pastors, monks, and nuns — lead prayers and blessings.

After a death, families observe six days of vigil, keeping doors and windows open, and ensuring that one family member stays awake each night, so the soul isn't alone.

A monk visits on the first day to pray and protect the spirit. Families offer food to monks in return for *parittas* (protective chants), hoping to safeguard the soul's journey. Homes keep lights on throughout the night in spiritual solidarity.

Note: Myanmar blends Theravada Buddhist rituals with traditional folk beliefs.

NEPAL

Gai Jatra / Śrāddha

IN NEPAL, THE DAY OF THE DEAD IS OBSERVED THROUGH *GAI JATRA* AND *Śrāddha*. *Gai Jatra*, or the "Festival of Cows," is held on the first day of the waning moon in the month of Bhadra (August–September). Families who have lost loved ones in the past year decorate a cow and lead it through the streets with music, dancing, and jokes. If a cow is unavailable, children dress as cows to represent the soul's guide.

Śrāddha is a private family ceremony honoring ancestors with prayers, fasting, offerings, and the wearing of white. The first death anniversary is known as *Barsy*. The 13-day mourning period, called *Kriya*, includes rituals and visits from extended family and friends.

These traditions, dating back to the Malla dynasty in the 17th century, remind families that death is a natural part of life.

NICARAGUA

Día de los Difuntos

IN NICARAGUA, *DÍA DE LOS DIFUNTOS* BEGINS ON NOVEMBER 1ST WITH *Día de los Angelitos* ("Day of the Little Angels") for deceased children, and November 2nd is for adults.

Families begin with Mass in the morning, followed by a full day at the cemetery, cleaning graves, lighting candles, and placing flowers and food offerings. Vendors sell snacks and drinks, and Mariachi bands perform music for both the living and the dead.

At home, families build altars (*ofrendas*), adorned with photos, papel picado, candles, and food like *pan de muertos*. Faces are painted, skull masks worn, and stories are shared to honor and connect with the souls of their ancestors.

NIGER

Ethnic and Religious Mourning Traditions

IN NIGER, MOURNING CUSTOMS VARY AMONG ITS MAJOR ETHNIC groups—Hausa, Zarma, and Tuareg—and are shaped by Islamic, Christian, and traditional animist beliefs. For most Hausa and Zarma families, funerals follow Islamic rites, including the ritual washing of the body, wrapping it in a *kafan* (white shroud), Janazah prayers, and burial facing Mecca, often on the same day.

Following the burial, families observe three-, seven-, and forty-day commemorations, gathering to recite Qur'anic verses, share meals, and pray for the soul's peace. Some also prepare the deceased's favorite foods to share with guests as a sign of remembrance and hospitality.

Among Tuareg communities, mourning may include chants, poetry, storytelling, and ritual blessings by elders. Items like personal belongings or symbols of the deceased may be left at the burial site, and mourners may wear black or white for extended periods to honor the dead.

Across traditions, families may clean graves, lay flower petals, and light lamps or incense. While many believe in judgment and paradise through Islam, others still hold to ancestral return or spiritual reincarnation, especially in rural or nomadic areas.

NORWAY

Allehelgendag

IN NORWAY, *ALLEHELGENDAG* ("ALL SAINTS' DAY") IS THEIR DAY OF THE Dead, observed on the first Sunday of November. It is a Norwegian Church holiday commemorating the deceased.

Families visit cemeteries, place flowers and candles, and sing psalms at gravesites. During funeral services, short speeches are given by loved ones, and children may sing songs to raise money for school.

As a final farewell, carpenters seal the coffin, often nailing wreaths to the lid. The burial ceremony is considered both a solemn and hopeful day.

Panama

Día de los Muertos

IN PANAMA, *DÍA DE LOS MUERTOS* IS CELEBRATED ON NOVEMBER 1ST FOR children (*Día de los Angelitos*) and November 2nd for adults. Families begin the day with Mass, followed by visits to cemeteries.

Graves are cleaned and decorated with flowers, and families gather at home to share stories and memories. The Rezo del Rosario (Rosary prayer) is held in the evening, with a white cloth-covered cross, flowers, candles, and a glass of water placed as offerings.

The family keeps vigil overnight, sharing memories until a second Mass is held the next day, followed by burial. It is a quiet, respectful day — alcohol sales and loud music are prohibited.

Paraguay

Día de los Muertos

IN PARAGUAY, *DÍA DE LOS MUERTOS* IS OBSERVED ON NOVEMBER 1ST AS *Día de los Angelitos* and November 2nd for adults. Families spend hours or the whole day at the cemetery, decorating graves with candles, candy, and white scarves.

Stories, jokes, and laughter fill the air, turning the day into a joyful celebration of life.

At home, families build altars (*ofrendas*) with food, drinks, calaveras (skulls), papel picado, and marigold flowers. Paths of flowers may be made from the cemetery to the house to guide spirits home.

Traditional foods like *pan de muertos*, *atole*, *pozole*, and *elote* are prepared. The iconic figure of *La Catrina* — a tall skeleton woman with a feathered hat — is also part of the celebration.

PERU

Día de los Difuntos

IN PERU, *DÍA DE LOS DIFUNTOS* IS CELEBRATED ON NOVEMBER 1ST FOR children (*Angelitos*) and November 2nd for adults. Families build *ofrendas* at home and in public, filled with food, drinks, candles, and photos of the deceased.

At cemeteries, graves are decorated, and families often spend the night beside their loved ones with candles burning, music, and food offerings.

A popular food is *T'antawawa* (also spelled *tantawawa*), a sweet bread shaped like a baby (for girls) or a horse (for boys), meant to symbolize life and remembrance.

The Cementerio de Nueva Esperanza in Lima becomes a massive celebration site, one of the largest cemeteries in the world, transformed into a gathering of music, family, and remembrance.

Philippines

Undas

IN THE PHILIPPINES, *UNDAS* IS THE DAY OF THE DEAD, OBSERVED ON November 1st and 2nd. It is also known as *Araw ng mga Yumao*, *Todos los Santos*, or *All Saints' Day*, reflecting its Roman Catholic roots.

Families visit cemeteries to clean and decorate graves with flowers and candles, bringing favorite foods of the deceased such as *pancit*, *caldereta*, *puto*, *kakanin*, *biko*, *cassava cake*, and *calamares*. Families may stay overnight at the cemetery, keeping their loved ones company by sharing stories, playing games, and eating together. White flowers are placed to symbolize solemnity and remembrance.

POLAND

Zaduszki

IN POLAND, *ZADUSZKI* IS THE DAY OF THE DEAD, CELEBRATED ON NOVEMBER 1st and 2nd. The name comes from *Dzień Zaduszny*, meaning "the day of prayers for souls." The tradition blends Catholic belief with folk customs that the spirits return to earth.

Families attend Mass and visit cemeteries, lighting candles, placing flowers, and praying especially for souls in purgatory. Some prepare bread offerings for the poor or clergy and leave them at the graves. Priests often walk through the cemetery, blessing graves with holy water.

PORTUGAL

Dia dos Fiéis Defuntos / Pão-por-Deus

IN PORTUGAL, *DIA DOS FIÉIS DEFUNTOS* IS OBSERVED ON NOVEMBER 2ND, the day after *Todos os Santos* (*All Saints' Day*) on November 1st. While not officially called a Day of the Dead, the occasion serves a similar purpose — a time for families to honor and remember deceased loved ones.

Families attend Mass and then visit cemeteries to clean graves, leave chrysanthemums, and light candles. Children take part in a beloved tradition called *Pão-por-Deus* ("Bread for God"), going door to door reciting verses and receiving nuts, sweets, fruit, or homemade bread. In some regions, this is also called *Bolinho* or *Santoro*.

Traditional treats include dried figs, roasted chestnuts, raisin sweetbreads, and honeyed almonds, often shared in memory of the departed. While not somber in tone, the day is observed with quiet reverence and family reflection.

Note: Though Portugal does not call this a "Day of the Dead," its observances of *Dia dos Fiéis Defuntos* and *Pão-por-Deus* serve a comparable purpose, particularly in rural and religious communities. The tradition of *Pão-por-Deus* is linked to the aftermath of the 1755 Lisbon earthquake.

Puerto Rico

Día de los Muertos

IN PUERTO RICO, *DÍA DE LOS MUERTOS* IS CELEBRATED ON NOVEMBER 1ST and 2nd. The first day, *Día de los Angelitos*, honors deceased children. Families create altars with toys, food, and candles. On November 2nd, adults are honored with *altares* decorated with photos, flowers, sugar skulls, skeletons, and the deceased's favorite food and drinks.

Pan de muertos is baked and decorated with white frosting to resemble bones. Families dress as *Catrinas*, wear skull makeup, and celebrate with music, fireworks, and food, believing the dead return to visit. Mass is held at cemeteries for *Los Fieles Difuntos*, and candles are lit for seven days as part of Catholic tradition to help souls leave purgatory.

ROMANIA

Ziua Morților

IN ROMANIA, *ZIUA MORȚILOR* IS THE DAY OF THE DEAD, OBSERVED ON November 2nd. Families visit cemeteries, light candles, and decorate graves with flowers and wreaths to guide spirits to the afterlife.

They bring food and share meals at the cemetery, distributing items to others in the spirit of remembrance. Traditional offerings include *coliva* (sweet boiled wheat), *pomul* (symbolizing the tree of life), and gifts for the poor. The ritual *bochirea* (mourning chants) is performed morning, afternoon, and evening.

Russia

Radonitsa

IN RUSSIA, *RADONITSA* (ALSO SPELLED *RADUNITSA* OR *RADONICA*) IS observed on the Tuesday after Orthodox Easter and honors the memory of the deceased. Families visit graves to share meals, bring dyed eggs, and recite blessings, transforming mourning into celebration.

A glass of vodka and black bread may be left at home as an offering to the soul. Orthodox funerals are typically held on the third day after death, with bells rung from high to low tones. Widows may wear black for years, and some traditions include priests, pastors, or rabbis depending on faith. The greeting, "May their memory be eternal," reflects the belief in life after death.

RWANDA

Ikiriyo

IN RWANDA, *IKIRIYO* IS A MOURNING PERIOD THAT LASTS THREE TO SEVEN days. Family and friends gather at the deceased's home to share stories, light a fire, and pay respects.

A family member prepares the body while others collect personal items to bury with the deceased. At the grave or home, the *gukaraba* ("washing of hands") ceremony is performed as a final act of remembrance. The color purple symbolizes mourning, and a pitcher of water and a framed photo of the deceased may be placed nearby.

Saint Vincent

Día de los Muertos

IN SAINT VINCENT, FUNERALS ARE LIVELY EVENTS WITH MUSIC, BANDS, and parades celebrating the journey of the deceased. At home, families set up *altares*, *ofrendas*, or shrines, decorated with photos, food, drinks, calaveras, and candles.

Marigolds are placed at the cemetery, papel picado banners wave in the wind, and candles form a cross on graves. Families gather to eat, tell stories, and celebrate life, blending Catholic tradition with Caribbean influences.

SAMOA

Fiafia

IN SAMOA, *FIAFIA* IS A CELEBRATION OF LIFE, OFTEN PART OF MULTI-DAY funerals. These gatherings include dancing, singing, prayers, and hymns, reflecting both ancestral customs and Christian traditions. A funeral song like *Mo'omo'oga* ("Saying Goodbye") may be sung during the ceremony.

A *tulafale* (talking chief) leads the funeral, telling stories about the deceased and offering final words. Families exchange *fa'alavelave* — ceremonial gifts — to show love, support, and unity.

The core of Samoan belief is *Fa'a Samoa* ("The Samoan Way"), which emphasizes respect for elders, ancestors, and spiritual presence. Death is seen as a passage, not an end, and the family (*aiga*) gathers to honor that transition.

Note: "Fiafia" usually refers to festive gatherings, not specifically to funerals, though it is used in memorial contexts.

SERBIA

Zadušnice (Serbian All Souls' Day)

IN SERBIA, *ZADUŠNICE* IS A RELIGIOUS DAY TO HONOR THE DEAD, OBSERVED four times a year, once per season. Saturday is the traditional day devoted to the dead. Early in the morning, families visit cemeteries to light candles, offer food, and say prayers.

Before the visit, families prepare *slavski kolač* (ritual bread) which is blessed at church. At the grave, it is shared with the deceased. Red eggs may also be placed on the grave, symbolizing resurrection and remembrance.

A priest walks through the cemetery, offering blessings as families share meals, stories, and remember loved ones. Serbian culture emphasizes honoring ancestors, especially among Orthodox Christian families.

Slovakia

All Saints' Day / Dušičky

IN SLOVAKIA, *ALL SAINTS' DAY (SVIATOK VŠETKÝCH SVÄTÝCH)* IS OBSERVED on November 1st, followed by *Dušičky* (*Little Souls' Day*) on November 2nd. Families visit cemeteries to light candles, lay chrysanthemums, and pray for the dead.

This tradition combines Catholic and Eastern Christian practices, dating back to the 4th century. Graves are carefully cleaned and decorated, and the entire cemetery becomes a sea of lights and flowers.

After visiting, families often walk the cemetery paths, sharing memories, and offering quiet reflection. Some tears are shed, but laughter often follows as stories of the deceased are retold with affection.

Slovenia

Dan Mrtvih (Day of the Dead)

IN SLOVENIA, *DAN MRTVIH* IS CELEBRATED ON NOVEMBER 1ST AND IS ALSO known as *All Saints' Day*. Families begin preparing days in advance, cleaning graves and placing chrysanthemums.

Cemeteries are illuminated with deep red candles, creating a solemn atmosphere. A priest blesses the graves, and families observe moments of silence before sharing a meal with other families, often at the gravesite or back home.

The holiday blends Catholic observance with local customs rooted in community and remembrance.

Spain

Día de Todos los Santos / Día de los Difuntos

IN SPAIN, THE SEASON OF REMEMBRANCE BEGINS ON OCTOBER 31ST WITH *Día de las Brujas* (Day of the Witches), followed by *Día de Todos los Santos* (All Saints' Day) on November 1st, and *Día de los Difuntos* (All Souls' Day) on November 2nd.

Families visit cemeteries, bringing flowers, candles, bread, and even spicy chocolate or *atole*. Altars (*ofrendas*) are built at home or at graves, decorated with *pan de ánimas*, *papel picado*, sugar skulls, and photos.

Traditional sweets include *buñuelos de viento*, *huesos de santo*, *panellets*, and *castañas asadas*. Children may hear the tale of *La Catrina*, the elegant skeleton lady created by José Guadalupe Posada.

The play "Don Juan Tenorio" by José Zorrilla is traditionally performed around this time, exploring themes of sin, death, and redemption.

Note: Altars and sugar skulls are more common in Latin American practice, though cross-cultural influence is growing.

Sri Lanka

Mataka Danes, Mala Batha, and Mataka Vastra Puja

IN SRI LANKA, VARIOUS BUDDHIST AND HINDU TRADITIONS ARE OBSERVED to honor the dead. *Mataka Danes* is performed seven days, three months, and one year after death to ward off bad spirits and bring peace to the soul.

Mala Batha is a ritual meal offered after burial or cremation. Families tie white flags on fences and poles to guide the spirit home. Monks lead chanting rituals and blessings at home and cemetery.

An important custom is *Mataka Vastra Puja*, the offering of new cloth to monks on behalf of the deceased. Someone must always be present with the body overnight, so the spirit is never alone.

SUDAN

Sadaga

IN SUDAN, *SADAGA* REFERS TO A GATHERING HELD IN REMEMBRANCE OF the dead on the 7th and 40th day after death. Families visit graves with prayers, singing, and food offerings like fattah, baleela, and nasha (a fermented sorghum drink).

Before burial, the body undergoes *ghusl* (ritual washing), wrapped in a *kafan*, and taken to the mosque for *Salat al-Janazah* (funeral prayer). At the cemetery, family and friends cry, sing, and dance to ease the spirit's transition to the afterlife.

Sudanese belief emphasizes that spirits remain present, and death is ordained by God, linking both Islamic and ancestral views in their mourning practices.

SURINAME

Broko Dey and Ancestral Mourning

IN SURINAME, FUNERAL TRADITIONS REFLECT THE COUNTRY'S DIVERSE ethnic groups — including Javanese, Indo-Surinamese, Creole, and Maroon communities. On the evening before the funeral, families hold a night wake called *broko dey* or *singi neti*, beginning at 8 p.m. and ending at dawn. This event includes storytelling, singing, and prayers, reflecting the belief that death is a passage to a different form of life.

The concept of *levende-doden* ("living-dead") expresses the idea that the deceased continue to influence the living. Many believe in *Winti* (spiritual afterlife) and *Ndyuka* (reincarnation), where the spirits of the righteous return as infants. A farewell dance called the *Krepsi-step* is performed to confuse evil spirits before burial.

Eight days after the funeral, families gather for *aiti dey*, a final farewell where loved ones sing, share stories, and honor the spirit of the deceased. This is part of a tradition called *dede sos*, meaning "home of the dead," which highlights the lasting connection between the living and the ancestors.

SWEDEN

Alla Helgons Dag (All Saints' Day)

IN SWEDEN, *ALLA HELGONS DAG* IS CELEBRATED ON THE SATURDAY between October 31 and November 6. Although not called Day of the Dead, it shares many similarities. Families visit cemeteries, lighting candles and placing wreaths to honor their departed. These candles are left glowing all weekend, turning graveyards into fields of flickering light.

The two-day observance, known as *allahelgonashelgen*, includes All Saints' Day and All Souls' Day. Many families visit Skogskyrkogården in Stockholm, a UNESCO World Heritage cemetery with five chapels, to pay respects. It is a time for quiet reflection, remembering loved ones with solemnity and warmth.

SWITZERLAND

Totensonntag (Sunday of the Dead)

IN SWITZERLAND, *TOTENSONNTAG* — ALSO CALLED *EWIGKEITSSONNTAG* (Eternity Sunday) — is observed on the last Sunday before Advent. It's a Protestant day of remembrance for the faithful departed. Families visit cemeteries, bring chrysanthemums, and sometimes play music or share meals near the graves of their loved ones.

In older Swiss traditions, people believed the living and the dead mingled in late October and early November. Some rural customs included removing a home's roof so the soul could rise to heaven, and carrying lemons in one's hat to ward off spirits — placing them on the grave for good luck.

Note: The "lemon in the hat" tradition is anecdotal and not broadly practiced today; likely regional folklore.

SYRIA

Khamis al-Amwat (Thursday of the Dead)

IN SYRIA, *KHAMIS AL-AMWAT* IS OBSERVED THREE DAYS BEFORE EASTER Sunday. Known as "Thursday of the Dead" or "Thursday of the Eggs," families — both Christian and Muslim — visit cemeteries in the early morning to pray for the departed. Women often lead this tradition, bringing bread cakes known as *ka'ak al-asfar* (yellow rolls), dried fruits, and painted eggs to distribute to the poor and children.

This observance has roots in medieval Christian and local Near Eastern beliefs, emphasizing the bond between the living and the dead. Tomb visits are followed by prayers, song, and processions led by rural villagers (*fellaheen*), varying by region.

TAIWAN

Qingming Festival

TAIWAN'S *QINGMING FESTIVAL*, **ALSO KNOWN AS TOMB-SWEEPING** Day, is celebrated in early April. Families visit graves to clean and decorate them with flowers, food, and incense. They burn *joss paper* and symbolic paper goods as offerings to ancestors. Games, kite-flying, and picnics at cemeteries reflect the festive yet reverent spirit of the day.

Another significant event is the Ghost Festival on the 15th day of the 7th lunar month. On this day, families honor *"good brothers and sisters"* — wandering souls without living relatives — by setting up street altars with food and incense. Doors and windows are left open to welcome spirits, and paper money is burned to ensure a comfortable afterlife.

Thailand

Boon Para Wate & Sart Duen Sip

IN THAILAND, HONORING THE DEAD TAKES PLACE DURING FESTIVALS LIKE *Boon Para Wate* and *Sart Duen Sip*. *Boon Para Wate* occurs between May and July and includes parades with colorful costumes, music, and playful acts to mock evil spirits. On the third day, families go to temples to hear Buddhist sermons and reflect on mortality.

Sart Duen Sip, observed in the 10th lunar month, is a solemn occasion when families make food offerings at temples for deceased ancestors. A symbolic *three-tail funeral banner* is often used to guide the spirit upward. In some rituals, banners are shaped into *wada* (angels), representing the soul's rebirth in heaven.

TIMOR-LESTE

Haha Metan

IN TIMOR-LESTE, *HAHA METAN*, MEANING "BLACK WORDS," IS A traditional mourning rite. After a person dies, families stay in the home for two weeks, praying, mourning, and lighting candles. During the funeral, loved ones walk beside the coffin, sing hymns, and place flowers on the grave.

After burial, families gather again to say the names of the deceased aloud and honor their ancestors. *Haha Metan* is observed every year to mark the anniversary of a loved one's death and reflects the blend of Indigenous beliefs and Catholic practices in separating the worlds of the living and the dead.

TRINIDAD AND TOBAGO

All Saints Day, Faithful Departed Day,
Día de Todos los Santos y Los Fieles Difuntos

IN TRINIDAD AND TOBAGO, SEVERAL TRADITIONS HONOR THE DEAD, including *All Saints Day*, *Faithful Departed Day*, and *Nine-Night* (a wake held nine days after death, especially when families return from other islands). Families create altars, or *ofrendas*, at home or at the gravesite, decorating them with photos, mementos, and the deceased's favorite foods, inviting the spirits to share a meal.

The four elements of nature represent the journey to the next world: earth (food to feed the souls), wind (to move objects), water (to quench thirst), and fire (candlelight to guide forgotten souls). Decorative elements may include *catrinas*, *catrins*, sugar skulls (*calaveras de azúcar*), *cempasúchil* flowers, papel picado, and other handmade skeletons.

TONGA

Pongipongi tapu

IN TONGA, *PONGIPONGI TAPU* MEANS "SACRED MORNING." WHEN A LOVED one dies, families hold a taumafa kava or royal kava ceremony. Homes are decorated with purple drapes and black cloth on fences to signify mourning, and these decorations are traditionally kept up for one year.

At the gravesite, families drink kava, bring flowers and food, and share stories about the deceased. On the birthdays of the dead, family members wear a ta'ovala (a woven mat wrapped around the waist) to signify loss. The atmosphere is solemn, with religious hymns replacing love songs.

TURKEY

Mevlit

IN TURKEY, A MEVLIT CEREMONY IS HELD TO HONOR A PERSON'S LIFE AND death. Before burial, the body is wrapped in a white cloth and positioned toward Qibla (the direction of Mecca). Burial occurs soon after death. A red wreath marks a woman's grave; a flag is used for men or soldiers.

Mourning rituals are observed on the 3rd, 7th, 40th, and 52nd days after death. At the cemetery, families pray, recite the Qur'an, and share food. Candles and incense are burned, and lights are left on to prevent evil spirits from entering the house.

UKRAINE

Provody

IN UKRAINE, *PROVODY* IS OBSERVED AFTER EASTER SUNDAY TO REMEMBER the dead. Families go to church and then to the cemetery to clean graves, place flowers, and bring food for the deceased—which is also shared with the needy. The belief is that the dead join the living for this communal meal.

There are five remembrance milestones: the 3rd, 9th, 40th day, and at six months and one year. A traditional dish is *kolach*, a braided bread served both at home and the cemetery. Incorrect observance of rituals is believed to bring misfortune.

United States

Day of the Dead / Día de los Muertos

IN THE UNITED STATES, *DÍA DE LOS MUERTOS* IS INCREASINGLY celebrated, especially in Latino communities. Rooted in Aztec tradition, the belief is that the dead do not disappear but continue to care for the living. November 1st is for children (*Día de los Angelitos*), and November 2nd is for adults. Families build altars (*ofrendas*) with photos, favorite foods, drinks, and Pan de Muertos. Graves are decorated with marigolds (*cempasúchil*), candles, and offerings.

Participants paint their faces as *calaveras* (skulls), create sugar skulls, and attend parades and festivals with mariachi music. Popular films such as *Spectre* (2015) and *Coco* (2017) helped popularize the holiday across the U.S.

URUGUAY

Día de los Muertos

IN URUGUAY, *DÍA DE LOS MUERTOS* IS CELEBRATED ON NOVEMBER 1ST *(DÍA de los Angelitos)* for children and November 2nd for adults. The tradition dates back to the 18th-century colonial period. Families create *ofrendas* at home, public spaces, or gravesites with photos, candles, food, and *Pan de Muertos*, inviting the spirits to return.

Common observances include face painting, visiting cemeteries, and preparing favorite meals of the dead. These rituals help preserve memory and familial connection.

UZBEKISTAN

Seeing-Off to the Last Journey

IN UZBEKISTAN, FUNERALS FOLLOW ISLAMIC TRADITION. WOMEN DO not attend cemetery burials; only men accompany the deceased. A mullah performs the *janoza* (funeral prayer), and a person asks, "What type of person was he or she?" The traditional response is, "A good and worthy person is going to Eden."

Mourning rituals take place on the 7th, 20th, 40th, and 365th days after death. A memorial meal is held 40 days or one year later. Families hang the deceased's clothes at home, and meals are prepared outside by relatives. The soul is believed to live on through good deeds.

VENEZUELA

Día de los Difuntos

IN VENEZUELA, *DÍA DE LOS DIFUNTOS* IS OBSERVED ON NOVEMBER 1ST for children (*Día de los Angelitos*) and November 2nd for adults. Families visit graves, clean them, and leave flowers, candles, and food the deceased enjoyed. Families often prepare their visits in advance.

Día de Todos Santos (All Saints' Day) is also celebrated on November 2nd. At night, families gather in cemeteries, light candles, and stay with their deceased, avoiding grief in favor of peaceful remembrance.

VIETNAM

Ngày giỗ

IN VIETNAM, *NGÀY GIỖ* IS THE ANNUAL DEATH ANNIVERSARY OF A FAMILY member. It translates to "an invitation to spirits" and is a day to remember and celebrate the lives of deceased loved ones. The eldest son is typically responsible for organizing the memorial feast and worship rituals. The meal includes boiled chicken, stir-fried dishes, steamed or fried shrimp, soup, and rice. Incense sticks are burned at the start of the offering, inviting the spirits to return home and be honored.

Before the *Tết* holiday, families observe *Lễ Thanh Minh*, a tradition of grave cleaning and incense offering, symbolizing respect for ancestors. *Đám giỗ* is the family gathering during the death anniversary, when offerings are made, and relatives visit pagodas and homes to pray and remember the deceased. Another custom, *Thanh Minh*, observed on the third day of the third lunar month, involves visiting ancestral graves, praying, and offering cold food. These rites express deep respect for familial lineage and spiritual continuity.

Vietnamese people believe that while the body dies, the soul continues to exist in another realm. In late August or early September (during the Ghost Festival, known locally as *Tết Trung Nguyên*), it is believed that ancestral spirits return home to visit their descendants.

CONCLUSION

DAY OF THE DEAD, OR DÍA DE LOS MUERTOS, IS MORE THAN JUST A tradition—it is a heartfelt reminder that even in death, our loved ones remain close to us. For seven days, families around the world pause to remember those who have passed. It is a time to honor their memory not with sorrow, but with love, gratitude, and celebration. Through shared meals, prayers, music, and stories, the living keep the spirit of the deceased alive. This celebration focuses not just on mourning the loss, but on celebrating the lives once lived.

As seen throughout this book, by exploring the different yet similar customs across many countries, we learn how families gather in homes, cemeteries, and sacred spaces to build *ofrendas* (altars), prepare favorite foods, and decorate with *calaveras* (skulls) and *Pan de Muertos* (bread of the dead).

The history of Day of the Dead can be traced back more than 3,000 years to the rituals of Indigenous peoples who believed that the dead coexisted with the living. That belief still holds true today. Around the world, people mark these days as sacred, recognizing the cycle of life and death as part of their cultural identity.

Once a year, it is said, the souls of the departed return—not to haunt, but to be with their families again. For a brief moment, the veil is lifted, and the past and present meet around the table, at the altar, and in the

heart. In that spirit, Day of the Dead continues to grow—not only as a tradition, but as a celebration of connection, remembrance, and the unbreakable bond between the living and the dead.

May these pages serve as an invitation to reflect, to honor, and to remember—wherever you are, and whoever you hold dear. The journey of remembrance is one we share across cultures, across time, and across generations.

About the Author

THE AUTHOR PROUDLY SERVED 20 YEARS in the United States Air Force, with 14 of those years spent overseas. During his military career, he completed two tours in Southeast Asia. His first tour was in South Vietnam, where he was assigned to the Military Assistance Command, Vietnam – Special Operations Group (MACV-SOG). Following his service in Vietnam, he was stationed at U-Tapao, Thailand, in support of "Operation Linebacker II."

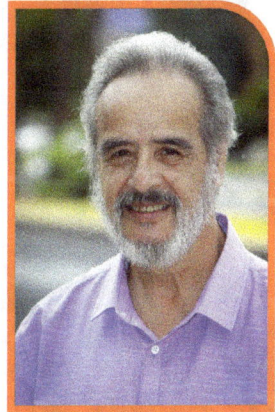

After retiring from the Air Force in 1988 with the rank of Master Sergeant, he relocated to Mesa, Arizona, to complete his education in Library Science. He subsequently began his civilian career at the Maricopa Community College District Library, working in Library Technical Services (LTS).

He was an active member of the Arizona Association of Chicanos for Higher Education (AACHE), where he served on the interview committee for the 27th Annual Conference, *Cultivating the Dream,* helping to award scholarships to Chicano and Chicana students throughout Arizona.

He is a lifetime member of Veterans of Foreign Wars (VFW) Post #9981 in Anchorage, Alaska, and a proud member of the American Legion, Tony F. Soza-Ray Martinez Thunderbird Post 41, in Phoenix, Arizona.

In addition to *Honoring Day of the Dead Around the World,* he is the author of three other works: *39 Years of Blue: A Collection of Life Stories, Hispanic Heritage and Participation on United States Stamps,* and *Latino Medal of Honor Recipients from 1864–2011.*